*Opposing
Viewpoints*®

OTHER BOOKS OF RELATED INTEREST

OPPOSING VIEWPOINTS SERIES

Abortion
America Beyond 2001
American Values
America's Victims
Biomedical Ethics
Civil Liberties
Constructing a Life Philosphy
Death & Dying
Hate Groups
Paranormal Phenomena
Politics in America
21st Century Earth

CURRENT CONTROVERSIES SERIES

The Abortion Controversy
Ethics
Free Speech
Politicians and Ethics

Opposing
Viewpoints®

Mary E. Williams, Book Editor

David L. Bender, *Publisher*
Bruno Leone, *Executive Editor*
Bonnie Szumski, *Editorial Director*
Brenda Stalcup, *Managing Editor*
Scott Barbour, *Senior Editor*

OPPOSING
VIEWPOINTS®
SERIES

Greenhaven Press, Inc., San Diego, California

Library of Congress Cataloging-in-Publication Data

Culture wars : opposing viewpoints / Mary E. Williams, book editor.
    p.   cm. — (Opposing viewpoints series)
    Includes bibliographical references and index.
    ISBN 1-56510-939-2 (lib. : alk. paper). —
    ISBN 1-56510-938-4 (pbk. : alk. paper)
    1. United States—Social conditions—1980– . 2. Culture—
United States. 3. Popular culture—United States. 4. Social problems—
United States. 5. United States—Social life and customs. I. Williams,
Mary E., 1960– . II. Series: Opposing viewpoints series
(Unnumbered)
HN59.2.C85 1999
306'.0973—dc21   98-28276
                                                                        CIP

Greenhaven Press, Inc., P.O. Box 289009
San Diego, CA 92198-9009

"CONGRESS SHALL MAKE NO LAW... ABRIDGING THE FREEDOM OF SPEECH, OR OF THE PRESS."

First Amendment to the U.S. Constitution

The basic foundation of our democracy is the First Amendment guarantee of freedom of expression. The Opposing Viewpoints Series is dedicated to the concept of this basic freedom and the idea that it is more important to practice it than to enshrine it.

CONTENTS

WHY CONSIDER OPPOSING VIEWPOINTS?

"The only way in which a human being can make some approach to knowing the whole of a subject is by hearing what can be said about it by persons of every variety of opinion and studying all modes in which it can be looked at by every character of mind. No wise man ever acquired his wisdom in any mode but this."

John Stuart Mill

In our media-intensive culture it is not difficult to find differing opinions. Thousands of newspapers and magazines and dozens of radio and television talk shows resound with differing points of view. The difficulty lies in deciding which opinion to agree with and which "experts" seem the most credible. The more inundated we become with differing opinions and claims, the more essential it is to hone critical reading and thinking skills to evaluate these ideas. Opposing Viewpoints books address this problem directly by presenting stimulating debates that can be used to enhance and teach these skills. The varied opinions contained in each book examine many different aspects of a single issue. While examining these conveniently edited opposing views, readers can develop critical thinking skills such as the ability to compare and contrast authors' credibility, facts, argumentation styles, use of persuasive techniques, and other stylistic tools. In short, the Opposing Viewpoints Series is an ideal way to attain the higher-level thinking and reading skills so essential in a culture of diverse and contradictory opinions.

In addition to providing a tool for critical thinking, Opposing Viewpoints books challenge readers to question their own strongly held opinions and assumptions. Most people form their opinions on the basis of upbringing, peer pressure, and personal, cultural, or professional bias. By reading carefully balanced opposing views, readers must directly confront new ideas as well as the opinions of those with whom they disagree. This is not to simplistically argue that everyone who reads opposing views will—or should—change his or her opinion. Instead, the series enhances readers' understanding of their own views by encouraging confrontation with opposing ideas. Careful examination of others' views can lead to the readers' understanding of the logical inconsistencies in their own opinions, perspective on why they hold an opinion, and the consideration of the possibility that their opinion requires further evaluation.

EVALUATING OTHER OPINIONS

To ensure that this type of examination occurs, Opposing Viewpoints books present all types of opinions. Prominent spokespeople on different sides of each issue as well as well-known professionals from many disciplines challenge the reader. An additional goal of the series is to provide a forum for other, less known, or even unpopular viewpoints. The opinion of an ordinary person who has had to make the decision to cut off life support from a terminally ill relative, for example, may be just as valuable and provide just as much insight as a medical ethicist's professional opinion. The editors have two additional purposes in including these less known views. One, the editors encourage readers to respect others' opinions—even when not enhanced by professional credibility. It is only by reading or listening to and objectively evaluating others' ideas that one can determine whether they are worthy of consideration. Two, the inclusion of such viewpoints encourages the important critical thinking skill of objectively evaluating an author's credentials and bias. This evaluation will illuminate an author's reasons for taking a particular stance on an issue and will aid in readers' evaluation of the author's ideas.

As series editors of the Opposing Viewpoints Series, it is our hope that these books will give readers a deeper understanding of the issues debated and an appreciation of the complexity of even seemingly simple issues when good and honest people disagree. This awareness is particularly important in a democratic society such as ours in which people enter into public debate to determine the common good. Those with whom one disagrees should not be regarded as enemies but rather as people whose views deserve careful examination and may shed light on one's own.

Thomas Jefferson once said that "difference of opinion leads to inquiry, and inquiry to truth." Jefferson, a broadly educated man, argued that "if a nation expects to be ignorant and free . . . it expects what never was and never will be." As individuals and as a nation, it is imperative that we consider the opinions of others and examine them with skill and discernment. The Opposing Viewpoints Series is intended to help readers achieve this goal.

David L. Bender & Bruno Leone,
Series Editors

Greenhaven Press anthologies primarily consist of previously published material taken from a variety of sources, including periodicals, books, scholarly journals, newspapers, government documents, and position papers from private and public organizations. These original sources are often edited for length and to ensure their accessibility for a young adult audience. The anthology editors also change the original titles of these works in order to clearly present the main thesis of each viewpoint and to explicitly indicate the opinion presented in the viewpoint. These alterations are made in consideration of both the reading and comprehension levels of a young adult audience. Every effort is made to ensure that Greenhaven Press accurately reflects the original intent of the authors included in this anthology.

INTRODUCTION

"The cultural left has made enormous inroads into the culture that can never entirely be rolled back."

Ellen Willis

"The conservatives have the upper hand in the battle of ideas."

Dinesh D'Souza

The phrase "culture wars" is derived from the German word *Kulturkampf*, which literally means "a struggle for the control of the culture." In late nineteenth-century Germany, chancellor Otto von Bismarck launched a *Kulturkampf* against the Roman Catholic church, expelling Jesuits from the country and passing laws that restricted the role of the church in education and politics. The German citizenry strongly opposed Bismarck, however, and he was forced to abandon the *Kulturkampf* in 1878.

In twentieth-century America, the phrase "culture wars" has similarly been used to describe conflicts among religious, political, and secular interests. The famous Scopes trial of 1925, for example, is considered by many historians to be the first significant battle in America's *Kulturkampf*—in this case, a conflict between religion and science. John T. Scopes, a science instructor in Tennessee, was found guilty of teaching Charles Darwin's theory of evolution, which at that time was considered a crime in his state. Although Scopes was convicted, his fine was small, and the Tennessee supreme court eventually overturned the verdict on a technicality. More importantly, claims former American Civil Liberties Union director Roger N. Baldwin, the trial was seen as a victory for liberal and pro-science forces because literal interpretations of the Bible were revealed as fallacious on the witness stand. Subsequently, Christian fundamentalist attempts to criminalize the teaching of evolution in other states were largely unsuccessful. Religious conservatism then passed through several decades of near-withdrawal from public life.

In the meantime, politically liberal ideals gained the upper hand. During the 1960s and 1970s, activists and legislators won several victories for the civil rights and women's rights movements. In 1964, for example, Congress passed a Civil Rights Act that prohibited job discrimination based on age, race, religion, gender, or national origin. This legislation had a tremendous impact on American culture: Racial segregation in public facilities was outlawed, affirmative action policies were implemented, and large numbers of women entered the paid workforce. While liberals generally view the 1960s and 1970s as watershed decades, conservatives often contend that the decline in the influence of traditional religious values during those years harmed American culture. They decry the 1962 Supreme Court decision outlawing state-sponsored school prayer, for instance, as well as the 1973 *Roe v. Wade* decision that legalized abortion in the first two trimesters of pregnancy.

The 1980s, however, witnessed an upsurge in conservatism as a broad majority of voters elected Ronald Reagan as president. Reagan, a right-wing Republican, took a firm stance against abortion and openly advocated a more conservative approach to politics and culture. His influence changed the tenor of national debate as conservative religious organizations such as Pat Robertson's Christian Coalition became politically and culturally influential. In 1992, presidential hopeful Pat Buchanan popularized the phrase "culture wars" in his campaign speech to the Republican National Convention. Addressing concerns over such issues as abortion, affirmative action, and arts funding, he proclaimed that conservatives must declare a cultural revolution—"a war for the nation's soul."

Buchanan sees the culture wars as a political and spiritual battle largely between liberal secular forces and conservative religious forces. In a similar vein, sociologist James Davison Hunter, the author of *Before the Shooting Begins: Searching for Democracy in America's Culture War*, defines the culture wars as ongoing public debates between two opposing camps. These debates occur between various "orthodox" and "progressive" interests, cutting across the realms of politics, religion, economics, popular culture, and education. In the late 1980s and early 1990s, for instance, controversies over censorship, obscenity, and the definition of acceptable cultural standards dominated headlines, the courts, and college campuses. One such dispute emerged over whether the federal government's National Endowment for the Arts should have funded an exhibition of the work of Robert Mapplethorpe, whose photographs sometimes depicted explicit homosexual acts. Another controversy arose over whether high school and college curricula should emphasize the intellectual traditions of Western civilization or adopt a multicultural approach to literature and history. Still another nationwide debate involved the question of whether single-parent families are as viable as traditional two-parent families for raising children.

By the late 1990s, some commentators and cultural observers had come to the conclusion that America's culture wars had largely been "won." Conservative New York University professor Herbert London, for example, believes that "the Left has won the culture war." He argues, with regret, that multiculturalism, political liberalism, and moral decline reign on college campuses and that American popular culture is becoming more "hedonistic, violent, and pornographic." On the other hand, Stanley Katz, president of the American Council of Learned Societies, contends that the right is the current victor in the culture wars. He points out that conservative commentators dominate the airwaves and the op-ed pages of national newspapers. Furthermore, Katz maintains, conservative ideas, such as the current criticism of affirmative action, have become mainstream. "If you ask what is liberalism these days, nobody wants to answer the question," asserts Katz. "They [the right] won a lot, in terms of the way people think about things." Feminist writer Ellen Willis, however, thinks that the question of who has won the culture wars depends on one's point of view: "If you're a conservative and you're measuring today's culture against the 50s, you've been completely devastated. And if you're a feminist and a cultural radical and measuring today against the 60s or early 70s, it's pretty depressing."

Other cultural analysts argue that the liberal-versus-conservative split is, at present, not as deep as many commentators have claimed. Paul DiMaggio, a Princeton University sociologist, studied several decades of survey data and discovered that there had been "no dramatic rise in polarization of public opinion on social issues" since the early 1970s. Examining attitudes on numerous controversies, DiMaggio found a significant division of opinion only on abortion. Rhys H. Williams, a sociology professor at Southern Illinois University, agrees with DiMaggio, arguing that the phrase "culture wars" is more descriptive of the actions of political activists and policymakers than of the general public. In Williams's opinion, "Apathy is the dominant feature of public opinion. That's why activists feel compelled to pitch their appeals in strident terms."

Politicians, religious leaders, sociologists, and educators have come to no single conclusion about the timbre of America's Kulturkampf. The authors in Culture Wars: Opposing Viewpoints offer a spectrum of opinion on this multifaceted topic in the following chapters: What Is the Nature of America's Culture Wars? Is American Culture in Decline? What Cultural Influences Benefit Society? Should Government Regulate Cultural Values? Analyzing the responses to these questions will give readers a broad contemporary overview of America's culturally driven debates.

CHAPTER 1

WHAT IS THE NATURE OF AMERICA'S CULTURE WARS?

CHAPTER PREFACE

In the United States, the term "culture wars" has often been used to describe societal conflicts in the arenas of religion and politics, including such controversial issues as abortion, race relations, homosexuality, and welfare reform. These conflicts tend to occur between two competing factions: right-wing traditionalists and left-wing progressives.

Several commentators assert, moreover, that politically conservative religious organizations—referred to as the religious right—have exacerbated the culture wars. Liberal rabbi Michael Lerner maintains that some Americans are drawn to the religious right because it claims to have solutions to what many believe is a cultural crisis resulting from the nation's spiritual emptiness and moral decline. Lerner grants that conservative religion has addressed this spiritual crisis by emphasizing the importance of familial and communal nurturing. However, he argues, conservatives have also encouraged people to wrongly fault certain groups for America's moral and cultural crisis: "African Americans, feminists, gays and lesbians, communists (and more recently, liberals), Jews, immigrants, and other minorities are blamed for disruptions of safety, security, and morality." The religious and political right's deflection of societal anger onto these groups has intensified cultural conflict, Lerner and other liberal commentators contend.

Other analysts argue that the religious right should not be blamed for provoking America's culture wars. Boston University professor Peter Berger asserts that religious conservatism, rooted in early American Protestantism, maintained a cultural stronghold during the nineteenth and early twentieth centuries. However, Berger points out, the countercultural revolution of the 1960s and the ensuing rise of liberal, non-religious elites promoted values that contrasted sharply with the ethics of traditional religion. Religious conservatives perceived this new liberal establishment as a threat to American culture. The religious right then emerged in the 1980s as a resistance movement to oppose liberal mores, he maintains. Berger contends that a lack of effective negotiation between religious conservatives and secular liberals—not the beliefs of the religious right—is the true cause of the intensifying culture war in the United States.

The nature of the social conflicts that comprise America's culture wars continues to be a subject of debate among scholars, political activists, and religious leaders. The authors in the following chapter offer informative commentaries on this complex topic.

"There is little doubt that we are in the midst of a culture war of great social and historical consequence, and thus the possibility of conflict and violence should not surprise us."

THE CULTURE WARS REFLECT THE POLARIZATION OF AMERICAN SOCIETY

James Davison Hunter

In the following viewpoint, James Davison Hunter defines the culture wars as the ongoing societal disputes over values-laden issues such as abortion, sexual harassment, homosexuality, race relations, arts censorship, and euthanasia. Public discussion of these issues, he contends, is occurring in the form of increasingly belligerent—and occasionally violent—debates between two opposing camps. Because each camp argues that its opponent's claims are extremist and dangerous, democracy suffers from the lack of a more moderate and complex understanding of today's controversies, Hunter points out. Hunter, a sociology professor at the University of Virginia in Charlottesville, is the author of Culture Wars: The Struggle to Define America and Before the Shooting Begins: Searching for Democracy in America's Culture War, from which this viewpoint is excerpted.

As you read, consider the following questions:

1. According to Hunter, in what way does the culture war involve a "politics of the body"?
2. In what way is cultural conflict antidemocratic, in Hunter's opinion?
3. According to the author, how are culture-wars issues reduced to caricatures?

E very generation has its struggles. People being what they
are, such struggles are inevitable. In this, of course, we are
hardly immune. But in our time, a large region of public contention has opened up that is peculiar for both its moral character and its historical significance.

Think about it for a moment.

At the very center of contemporary cultural conflict in our
society—the "culture war," as it has been called—are a cluster
of public issues concerned, ironically, with the most private of
all matters: the body. Controversies about abortion, sexual harassment, pornography, "vulgar" art or music, sex education,
condom distribution, homosexuality, AIDS policy, or euthanasia
and the "right to die" all trace back to the human body. Those
issues that do not relate to the body deal, more often than not,
with the social institutions that claim authority over the body
(family, church, school, law and the like). The body, it would
seem, is the underlying symbolic of the culture war. This being
the case, the politics of the culture war is, in large part, a politics
of the body.

But why the body?

Clearly the human body is more than just a biological organ-
ism. It also has social meaning and significance. In short, how
we understand the body—its functioning, its representation,
and its discipline—reveals a particular cultural understanding of
nature, what the so-called natural order of things will allow or
not allow, and human nature (what it means to be human). Indeed, as Michel Foucault has instructed us, the body is ultimately a reflection of, and a central metaphor for, the implicit
order that prevails in a civilization.

If the body is indeed a metaphor of the social order, then a
conflict over our understanding of the body—latent within all
of the issues just mentioned—signals a conflict about (if not a
turning point in) the ordering of our social life, and perhaps
civilization itself. This is why abortion, to mention the most
prominent case, has been and remains so deeply contested. The
controversy over abortion carries many layers of meaning, to be
sure, but at root it signifies different propositions about what it
means to be human. As such, the controversy contains within it
a metaphor for two different civilizational ideals in conflict.

AN EPOCH-DEFINING MOMENT

In this light we begin to see the significance of the contemporary culture war. Cumulatively, the various issues of cultural
conflict point to a deeper struggle over the first principles of

how we will order our lives together; a struggle to define the purpose of our major institutions, and in all of this, a struggle to shape the identity of the nation as a whole. In a broader historical perspective, however, this culture war may also mark an epoch-defining moment—although in what sense is still unclear. One thing, though, is certain: when cultural impulses this momentous vie against each other to dominate public life, tension, conflict, and perhaps even violence are inevitable.

Conflict and violence? This observation is not made lightly, if only because *culture wars always precede shooting wars*—otherwise, as Philip Rieff reminds us, the latter wars are utter madness: outbreaks of the most severe and suicidal efforts to escape the implications of any kind of normative order. Indeed, the last time this country "debated" the issues of human life, personhood, liberty, and the rights of citizenship all together, the result was the bloodiest war ever to take place on this continent, the Civil War. There is little doubt that we are in the midst of a culture war of great social and historical consequence, and thus the possibility of conflict and violence should not surprise us. The memory of the shooting murder of abortion provider Dr. David Gunn of Pensacola, Florida, in February 1993 should stick in our mind as a poignant symbol of just this.

DEMOCRACY AND CULTURAL CONFLICT

The question . . . is whether American democracy can face up to conflict of this subtlety, significance, and potential volatility. Can democratic practice today mediate differences as deep as these in a manner that is in keeping with the ideals set forth in the founding documents of the American republic? Or will one side, through the tactics of power politics, simply impose its vision on all others?

The question is not an idle one—for the simple reason that cultural conflict is inherently antidemocratic. It is antidemocratic first because the weapons of such warfare are reality definitions that presuppose from the outset the illegitimacy of the opposition and its claims. Sometimes this antidemocratic impulse is conscious and deliberate; this is seen when claims are posited as fundamental rights that *transcend* democratic process. The right to have an abortion and the right to life, for example, are both put forward as rights that transcend deliberation. Similarly opposing claims are made on behalf of gay rights, women's rights, the rights of the terminally ill, and so on.

More often than not, though, the antidemocratic impulse in cultural conflict is implicit in the way in which activists frame their positions on issues. This is what is meant by the popular phrase *political correctness*—a position is so "obviously superior", so "obviously correct", and its opposite is so "obviously out of bounds" that they are beyond serious discussion and debate. Indeed, to hold the "wrong" opinion, one must be either mentally imbalanced (phobic—as in *homophobic*—irrational, codependent, or similarly afflicted) or, more likely, evil. Needless to say, in a culture war, one finds different and opposing understandings of the politically correct view of the world.

ATTEMPTS TO DEFINE OPPOSING AGENDAS

Consider, by way of illustration, the way in which both sides of the cultural divide in America attempt to identify the other's agenda with the deadly authoritarianism of Germany's Third Reich. One is first tempted to dismiss such associations as the stuff of a cheap polemic merely intended to discredit one's opposition. But such associations are not only found in the purple prose of direct mail or in the sensationalism of demagogues. Below are two compelling statements made by serious intellectual players on—in this case—the issue of abortion. The first was made by novelist Walker Percy in a letter he wrote to the *New York Times* in 1988:

> Certain consequences, perhaps unforeseen, follow upon the acceptance of the principle of the destruction of human life for what may appear to be the most admirable social reasons.

> One does not have to look back very far in history for an example of such consequences. Take democratic Germany in the 1920s. Perhaps the most influential book published in German in the first quarter of this century was entitled *The Justification of the Destruction of Life Devoid of Value*. Its co-authors were the distinguished jurist Karl Binding and the prominent psychiatrist Alfred Hoche. Neither Binding nor Hoche had ever heard of Hitler or the Nazis. Nor, in all likelihood, did Hitler ever read the book. He didn't have to.

> The point is that the ideas expressed in the book and the policies advocated were the product not of Nazi ideology but rather of the best minds of the pre-Nazi Weimar Republic—physicians, social scientists, jurists, and the like, who with the best secular intentions wished to improve the lot, socially and genetically, of the German people—by getting rid of the unfit and the unwanted.

> It is hardly necessary to say what use the Nazis made of these ideas.

> I would not wish to be understood as implying that the re-

spected American institutions I have named [the New York Times, the American Civil Liberties Union, the National Organization for Women, and the Supreme Court] are similar to corresponding pre-Nazi institutions.

But I do suggest that once the line is crossed, once the principle gains acceptance—juridically, medically, socially—innocent human life can be destroyed for whatever reason, for the most admirable socioeconomic, medical, or social reasons—then it does not take a prophet to predict what will happen next, or if not next, then sooner or later. At any rate, a warning is in order. Depending on the disposition of the majority and the opinion polls—now in favor of allowing women to get rid of unborn and unwanted babies—it is not difficult to imagine an electorate or a court ten years, fifty years from now, who would favor getting rid of useless old people, retarded children, anti-social blacks, illegal Hispanics, gypsies, Jews . . .

Why not?—if that is what is wanted by the majority, the polled opinion, the polity of the time.

Consider now a second observation made by legal scholar Laurence Tribe:

The abortion policies of Nazi Germany best exemplify the potential evil of entrusting government with the power to say which pregnancies are to be terminated and which are not. Nazi social policy, like that of Romania, vigorously asserted the state's right to ensure population growth. But Nazi policy went even further. Following the maxim that "Your body does not belong to you," it proclaimed the utter absence of any individual right in the matter and made clear that abortion constituted a governmental tool for furthering Nazi theories of "Aryan" supremacy and genetic purity.

Nazi propaganda constantly emphasized the duty of "Aryans" to have large families. Family planning clinics were shut down, often on the ground of alleged ties with communism. The Third Reich made every effort to control contraception, ultimately banning the production and distribution of contraceptives in 1941. The state, largely at the behest of SS leader Heinrich Himmler, abandoned its commitment to "bourgeois" marriage and undertook to promote the "voluntary" impregnation of "suitable women." Allowances were paid to women, married or not, for having children.

Abortion and even its facilitation were, in general, serious criminal offenses in Nazi Germany; a network of spies and secret police sought out abortionists, and prosecutions were frequent. By 1943 the penalty for performing an abortion on a "genetically fit" woman was death; those on whose premises abortions were performed risked prison sentences.

Clearly more is involved in these two statements than mere rhetorical posturing. Each passage conveys a deep and well–thought out suspicion that their opponents embrace an authoritarianism that can only exist at the cost of human liberty and ultimately, perhaps, human life. The perception and the fear of this kind of authoritarianism, reinforced by the quest of both sides to force a *political* solution to these controversies, may be a measure of the extent to which democratic practice has become a thin veneer for the competing "will to power."

A Winner-Takes-All Mentality

According to the culture wars thesis, individuals on either side of the divide see their world view as absolute and the opposition's as illegitimate and "utterly alien to the American way." The "rights"-based emphasis of contemporary discourse along with the polarizing nature of modern public debate (fostered through sound-bite long news accounts and the inflammatory language of computerized direct mailings) serves to exacerbate the cultural chasm. The result is a climate where activists engage the battle with a winner-takes-all mentality and where the more nuanced voices of the "muddled middle" are eclipsed by the sensationalized pronouncements of the extremes. Pointing to the absolutized certainty with which the different sides hold to their positions, C. Taylor observes that "the very nature of the Kulturkampf resides in [the] certainty that only one solution is defensible." As a consequence the opposition is vilified and a rational search for common ground becomes increasingly untenable.

James L. Nolan, ed., *The American Culture Wars*, 1996.

Thus, on one side we hear Tim Stafford, a senior writer for *Christianity Today* "reluctantly praise" the "extremism" of the pro-life movement. Drawing wisdom from the abolitionist movement of the nineteenth century, he concludes that the Civil War (precipitated by the activism of the abolitionists) was ultimately justified because "the nation was redefined as one built on liberty and equality, not compromise." Shall we do the same with abortion or, say, homosexuality? On the other side of the cultural divide we hear Andrew Sullivan of the *New Republic* come to a similar conclusion: "The fracturing of our culture is too deep and too advanced to be resolved by anything but coercion; and coercion . . . is not a democratic option." Indeed!

To be sure, the exercise of state power, even if through conventional politics, can never provide any democratically sustainable solution to the culture war. We must come to terms with the underlying issues of these controversies at a deeper and more profound level. But in a vital democracy, the means to that end are serious public reflection, argument, and debate.

A SHOUTING MATCH

I have used the terms *discussion, debate,* and *argument* loosely in the past few pages to describe how much of the social conflict on the contemporary American scene takes shape. In fact, it would seem as though there is very little real discussion, debate, or argument taking place. Debate, of course, presupposes that people are talking *to* each other. A more apt description of Americans engaged in the contemporary culture war is that they only talk *at* or *past* each other. If it is true that antagonists in this cultural struggle operate out of fundamentally different worldviews, this would seem inevitable. Is it not impossible to speak *to* someone who does not share the same moral language? Gesture, maybe; pantomime, possibly. But the kind of communication that builds on mutual understanding of opposing and contradictory claims on the world? That would seem impossible. And then, too, there is not really much talking, even if it is only past one another. What is heard is rather more like a loud bellowing, in the clipped cadences of a shouting match.

The irony in the way we Americans contend over these issues is striking to say the least. America embodies the longest-standing and most powerful democracy in the world. The principles and ideals that sustain it, not to mention the very founding documents that articulate those ideals, are a source of national pride and a model that many nations around the world strive to imitate. Yet the actual manner in which democratic discussion and debate are carried out in this country has become something of a parody of those ideals: obnoxious, at the very least; dangerous at the worst. In short, the most important and consequential issues of the day are presented through (and all too often based upon) what amounts to slogan, cliché, and aphorism—observations and opinions rendered within a ten-second "sound bite" and manifestos published in the latest direct mail copy or in a paid political advertisement in the *New York Times.* To be honest one would have to admit that advocates on all sides of the issues contested are culpable. And so it is that grave social concerns about the status and role of women are fashioned as anti-family; ethical concerns about the act of abortion are labeled anti-choice; policies rooted in the desire to redress the agelong oppression of minorities are dismissed as quotas; people who are nervous about the social effects of affirmative action risk being called racist; the severe problems of the criminal justice system are represented by the pathos of a Willie Horton or Charles Manson; deep moral quandaries about homosexuality are reduced to pseudopsychoanalytic categories like homophobia; art that questions social mores is decried as smut or blasphemy; and the enduring work of generations of intellectuals and writers is dismissed as the sexist, racist, and heterosexist claptrap of dead white males. The cacophony that too often marks contemporary public "debate" skreighs on.

A War to Impose Consensus

The problem is not that positions on complex issues are reduced to caricatures, even if the latter are ugly and slanderous. In political discourse this has long been a practice. Rather, the problem is that democracy in America has evolved in such a way that public debate now rarely seems to get beyond these caricatures. Democratic discourse becomes a trade in accusation, an exchange in vilification, and all of this occurs in a context where the first principles of our life together are at stake. The discord taking place in public life, then, goes beyond mere political disagreement following the collapse of consensus over these matters. It is very much a war to impose a new consensus by virtually any political and rhetorical means possible.

What of the average American in all of this? Ordinary Americans greet the bellowing of what now passes as public "discourse" with an attitude something akin to dread. Indeed, there is an exhaustion that characterizes the national spirit when the controversies recur. Surely the rhetoric of public debate is more polarized than we are as a people. And so it is that many Americans wish that these battles would just go away.

Private life, of course, can be a refuge for us. Heaven knows that between finding and keeping a job, making ends meet, holding a marriage together, raising kids, and the like, we have enough to occupy our time and attention. But our biographies invariably intersect the skirmishes of the larger culture war. We are discriminated against in getting a job or in receiving a promotion, a teenage daughter becomes pregnant and pleads for an abortion, a nephew "comes out of the closet," a local group of citizens wants to remove the textbooks from the neighborhood school because they are not multicultural enough—and private life is no longer much of a refuge at all.

Little Diversity Exists in Public Debate

And so we find ourselves embroiled in controversy that we seem helpless to influence or change. The terms of the so-called debate have already been set for us by powers and processes over which we have no control. Thus, for all of the diversity of belief, opinion, and perspective that really does exist in America, diversity is not much represented in public debate. Rather than pluralism, democratic discourse tends to reflect the dualism of opposing extremes. Clearly most Americans do have opinions on the critical issues of our day, but most of the time those opinions conform to neither of the reigning positions. Indeed, the majority of voices that would dissent from either credo are for all practical purposes drowned out by the rhetoric of ideologues. Voices in the middle—of a perplexed or even a well-conceived ambivalence—are rarely if ever given a hearing. Here again, the life and spirit of democratic practice suffers.

"What is often identified as evidence for a culture war has more to do with ... activist rhetoric than the attitudes or actions of the body politic generally."

THE CULTURE WARS ARE LARGELY RHETORICAL

Rhys H. Williams

Rhys H. Williams, associate professor of sociology at Southern Illinois University in Carbondale, is coauthor of *A Bridging of Faiths: Religion and Politics in a New England City*. He is also the editor of *Culture Wars in American Politics: Critical Reviews*, from which the following viewpoint is adapted. Williams points out that the phrase "culture wars" is often used to describe the conflicts in opinion that liberals and conservatives have over various social issues such as abortion, homosexuality, welfare reform, and school prayer. However, he argues, these liberal-versus-conservative divisions are less polarized than many commentators have claimed. America's political institutions have a moderating effect on societal conflicts, Williams asserts, and the phrase "culture wars" characterizes the rhetoric of activists rather than an actual political cleavage in society.

As you read, consider the following questions:

1. According to Williams, how did the phrase "culture war" gain national recognition?
2. What is the "broad" version of the culture-wars idea, in the author's opinion?
3. In Williams's opinion, what should be done to encourage more people to become politically involved?

A bortion clinics are firebombed; Planned Parenthood workers are murdered; an art gallery owner is arrested for exhibiting Robert Mapplethorpe's photographs; a rap group is arrested on obscenity charges, the civil rights—or "special privileges"—of gays and lesbians are the subject of controversial referenda; and issues of multiculturalism, freedom of expression and "political correctness" divide many college campuses. To many Americans, this does not seem like politics as usual. These stories and others like them seem to indicate that a new and different type of political conflict has swept the nation.

This new conflict even gets its own sound bite. We are witnessing a "culture war," we are told. American politics is no longer about class, race or region; rather, the body politic is now rent by a cultural conflict in which values, moral codes and lifestyles are the primary objects of contention.

THE USE OF WAR METAPHORS

Patrick Buchanan brought the glare of the national spotlight to the phrase "culture war" when he used his address to the 1992 Republican National Convention to declare a "war for the nation's soul." That moment was both the apex and the nadir of a presidential campaign that styled itself as a moral crusade. Oliver North's 1994 Senate campaign in Virginia echoed those themes. Buchanan's 1996 campaign was no less crusade-like, and the war metaphors were even more prominent as partisans were advised to "lock and load" and "ride to the sound of the gunfire." Other Republican hopefuls, Pat Robertson's Christian Coalition and such "cultural warriors" as Rush Limbaugh, former Secretary of Education William Bennett, and James Dobson, director of Focus on the Family, have claimed there is an encompassing social divide over morality and values.

Not to be outdone rhetorically, much fund-raising literature for liberal causes uses culture-wars language with similar tones of alarm. The hallowed principles of journalistic, artistic and academic freedom are threatened, they argue, and only a stout defense of the barricades will prevent a "neo-McCarthy" backlash from overwhelming the social and political progress of the last few decades. The nation is threatened by "moral zealots" who want to dictate all manner of life choices according to their strict neo-Puritan prejudices.

Academic observers have also contributed to this view of American public life. The most developed, systematic and sweeping version of the idea of a culture war appeared in the 1991 book *Culture Wars: The Struggle to Define America*, by James Davison Hunter, a University of Virginia sociologist. Hunter portrayed contemporary politics as an increasingly uncivil and conflict-ridden arena split into two competing sides that have little in common but mutual antipathy. The book's tone of urgency and its copious use of war metaphors left many readers with the distinct impression that American politics was experiencing an irreversible decline.

IS THE CULTURE-WARS RHETORIC ACCURATE?

But let's pause for a moment and step back from this heated—or is it overheated?—rhetoric. Though there does seem to be a lot of incivility in politics, and no limit to the various soapboxes from which extreme views can be heard, Buchanan, North and others all ran *losing* campaigns. None of the other cultural warriors I have mentioned holds elective office. Apparently none reflects the views of a majority. Critics from the left and the right launch impassioned attacks on the "system," but at a basic level the system continues to rebuff them. Why?

If we unpack the culture-wars argument carefully, we will see that the answer rests in large part on the differences between the *institutions* of politics and government and the *social movements* that are the focus of the culture-wars rhetoric. The organizations of the New Christian Right may motivate highly committed activists to engage in picketing, letter-writing and petition-signing. But few elections are won from the margins, and the art of compromise continues to be the sine qua non of legislating.

Furthermore, the cultural conflict that is taking place is more complicated than the activists on either side tend to suggest. There are actually two versions of the "culture wars" idea— what I will call the "broad" and the "narrow" versions. Recent research points out that while "culture" plays a critical role in social divisions, the "culture wars" rhetoric is basically inaccurate. The notion of a culture war is plausible—and a "broad" version of the idea is useful. But if the idea is understood too narrowly, it does more to obscure than to clarify the situation.

THE "BROAD" NOTION OF CULTURE WARS

So what is the "broad" version of the notion of a culture war? First and most important, it calls attention to the fact that several of the most contentious and passionate issues in current politics revolve around what can be called "cultural" concerns. Political analysts often assume that politics is only about economic interests. Moreover, they assume that people who vote or act against their direct economic interests must in some way misperceive their own interests. But politics is more than just a matter of dividing the economic pie. Contrary to economistic, interest-based assumptions, the cultural and symbolic aspects of our lives are deep sources of political motivation. People act in ways that their economic interests alone simply would not predict. They vote against their interests, they risk jail in order to protest injustice, they voluntarily take on hardships in order to uphold moral principles they hold dear.

THE DANGERS OF WAR TALK

I regret the haunting title of James Davison Hunter's recent book: *Before the Shooting Begins*. Such rhetoric may sell books. But such rhetoric does little to foster an ambiance in which those Americans who are alienated from each other can seek reconciliation. Indeed, it reinforces the mindset of people like those extremists who laud the killing of abortion doctors and staff.

The vast majority of other Americans are not hostile toward evangelical Christians and are not ready to shoot anybody. We would be more accurate to portray the bulk of the American public not as belonging to two giant phalanxes of the Right and Left engaged in mortal combat, but as religious centrists, remaining to varying degrees committed to Judeo-Christian values and to First Amendment guarantees regarding freedom of religion. There are theaters of cultural warfare, but millions of Americans are not self-consciously enlisted soldiers in them.

John D. Woodbridge, *Christianity Today*, March 6, 1995.

Of course, people do not make up their moral principles out of thin air. The moral codes people live by come from somewhere, often from religious teachings or beliefs. One source of moral codes is what might be called "public culture." Public culture is composed of ideas and symbols that are widely shared, found in major societal institutions, and do not depend on any one person or one group for their existence. Public culture can shape people's assumptions about what the "good society" is, what we must do to achieve it and what constitutes a "moral" life. When one set of assumptions about what constitutes a moral society is incompatible with rival sets of assumptions, the potential for conflict is evident. Fundamental moral commitments may be at stake, creating conflict not just about one's individual life, but about the very nature of society.

The culture-wars thesis correctly brings to our attention the potential for societal conflict when rival and incompatible moral worldviews collide. When these worldview differences are aligned with other social distinctions—such as economic class, race, region or religion—competition can turn from civil politics to cultural war. India, Ulster, Bosnia and Sudan serve as potent reminders of just how volatile a mixture moral commitments and political differences can be.

Indeed, the broad version of "culture wars" is particularly relevant to American politics in large part because of religion's continuing vitality in American life. Religious belief and participation remain higher in the U.S. than in almost any other industrialized country. And religion continues to be an important part of American public culture. Even if that role is not as significant as it once was, many Americans continue to want their society and their politics infused with moral commitment. Thus, religion can be politically effective by motivating individuals to extreme actions or sacrifice—and by providing the ideas and organizations that spearhead reformist social movements. . . .

THE "NARROW" NOTION OF CULTURE WARS

Despite the fact that culture conflict is deeply ingrained in American politics (I am calling this the "broad" version of the culture-wars idea), the "narrow" version of the argument found in Hunter's book (and many activists' rhetoric) is clearly wrong.

There are two basic claims in Hunter's *CultureWars* that need to be noted. First, Hunter portrays all important political opinion as lined up along one continuum, the poles of which he labels "orthodox" and "progressive." The difference between the orthodox view and the progressive view is where the two sides turn for moral and social authority. The orthodox locate moral authority in transcendent, universal sources (which provide the truth), while the progressive find authority in society, human reason and the here and now. This difference is thought to express the basic division in public political culture. Opinions and attitudes that do not fit easily along this continuum are irrelevant.

Indeed, Hunter claims that opinions, ideas or people that do not align with the progressive-orthodox divide get pushed onto one side or the other as public culture forces people to take sides. An important dimension of this claim is Hunter's attendant position that political activism is largely a matter of small groups of activists who set the terms for public politics as well as grass-roots opinion.

Second, Hunter argues not only that political conflicts run along this single axis, but that political positions cluster around the two poles of that axis. That is, each worldview leads to a cluster of inherently related opinions on issues as varied as abortion, gay rights, welfare reform, school prayer and economic policy. This clustering of issues leads to polarization and conflict, perhaps even violence, because the two poles are grounded in uncompromisable moral worldviews.

Moreover, the polarization represents a significant realignment of social divisions. The orthodox-vs.-progressive polarization cuts across many of the social cleavages (such as race or class) that organized American politics in the past. In sum, the "narrow" version of the culture-wars idea is that incompatible worldviews (the orthodox vs. the progressive) force all significant political ideas and public attitudes on to one side of a polarized line. Conflict is inevitable, intractable and escalating.

Is there really only one crucial cultural divide in contemporary culture—that between an orthodox and progressive vision of moral authority? Is cultural conflict so thorough and so pervasive that our institutions have lost their ability to moderate it? Perhaps most important, is the cultural divide that Hunter claims shapes the conflict between political activists now spreading to the general public?

No Deep Divisions in Public Opinion

We can begin answering these questions by stating that it is clearly not true that a single continuum can capture American political opinions, attitudes or values. Nor is it the case that opinions cluster at the poles of the axes that divide American political culture. Surveys show repeatedly that a single axis with polarized-attitude clusters does not represent a majority of opinions. Further, with the exception of attitudes toward abortion, there is evidence that general public opinion is not polarizing at all.

In fact, survey research consistently shows that there are at least two dimensions of political attitudes: one for issues pertaining to economics and political power (what I'll call "justice" issues) and another one for issues of personal behavior and cultural symbolism (what I'll call "morality" issues). And in many cases these dimensions are not related to each other—that is, those who are "liberals" on one set of issues are not necessarily "liberals" on the other set of issues.

This finding suggests a fourfold distinction rather than a two-sided war. Some people are "libertarian" on troth morality and justice issues: they believe that government should not interfere in individuals' lives and that individual rights take precedence over collective needs. Other people are communalist on both types of issues: they favor government regulation of both economic and personal moral behavior. There are also those who are morality libertarians and justice collectivists (sounding much like Great Society Democrats), and those who are morality collectivists and justice libertarians (sounding very much like the current Republican coalition).

So the data on mass opinion do not reveal a culture war of polarized attitude clusters. But we must still consider Hunter's point about political activism being mostly a matter of "elites" or partisan activists. Indeed, it is the rhetoric used by activists that promotes the images of "war." After all, the rhetoric must resonate with some people or it would not continue to be so popular. Certainly there is an uncivil tone to much current political language—although I urge those tempted by nostalgia to read up on the language used in 19th-century American politics. Incivility is hardly new.

WHY ACTIVISTS USE WAR RHETORIC

Nonetheless, it is true that activists' attitudes are often more polarized than the general public's, and activists often express those attitudes in more uncompromising language than many people feel comfortable with. Hunter is on to something here. But is this rhetoric an accurate reflection of underlying worldviews and the opinions that spring from them, or is it a tool that activists find useful in trying to rally troops to their cause?

Political activists of all stripes have difficulty getting ordinary citizens to care about their issues, and if they do care, to act on them. A longstanding truism in political science is that apathy and a lack of interest are the dominant features of public opinion. Many Americans do not care much about—or care for—politics. The falling voting rate is well known and much discussed. According to one estimate, only 5 percent of the general public can be considered politically engaged beyond the level of voting, and thus termed "activist"; concomitantly, a solid 20 percent are resolutely apolitical. The remaining 75 percent can be mobilized and activated, but their interest is intermittent, depending on their own situations and the context in which issues come to their attention.

If movement partisans are to get portions of the public behind them, therefore, they must pitch their appeals in ways that garner attention *and* motivate action. This need to gain attention explains the activists' moral urgency and war rhetoric. Scholars of social movements have found that before people become politically active they need three particular types of understandings, or "frames" through which to view the issue at hand. First, people need to perceive a situation as an "injustice"—that something is morally wrong. Second, they need a sense of "identity"—that is, they need to be able to identify the victims and the villains who are responsible for the injustice. And third, people must have a sense of "agency," a feeling that their own involvement will make a difference.

War rhetoric obviously fits these three requirements. It names an issue of abiding moral seriousness, it identifies the good guys and the bad guys, and it implores people to get involved lest the cause be lost. Because of the need for a certain amount of the us-vs.-them approach, activist rhetoric easily escalates toward uncompromising portrayals of good and evil. That is what Hunter and others discovered in their narrow version of "culture wars"—the rhetoric of movement partisans trying to break through to the nonactive and prod them to action.

But this is not an ideological divide that pits half of America vs. the other half; this is the hype—the "pep talk"—of those who are trying to rally troops to their side. What is often identified as evidence for a culture war has more to do with the requirements of activist rhetoric than the attitudes or actions of the body politic generally.

How to Avoid Further Polarization

Do some people talk in "culture war" terms? Of course they do. Is that talk a good guide to the worldviews, values or opinions of the public? Clearly not. In sum, the narrow version of the culture-war idea ignores the crucial difference between social-movement mobilizing and institutional politics.

While it may be comforting to know that America is not as divided or as unreasonable as the narrow culture-war thesis suggests, that does not make the current state of American politics any easier to take. Many people feel that their involvement is useless. Further, the stridency of much public culture no doubt discourages many people from involvement, even if they do care about an issue. I find myself turning off news programs when I feel that all I am hearing are the prefabricated ideological sound bites of spokespersons from interest groups. What can be done about this? If we care about our collective political life, and want as many people as active in public decision-making as possible—which is, after all, part of the definition of democracy—how do we avoid this cycle of polarizing activist rhetoric, public indifference and a resulting escalation of rhetoric?

Before addressing such questions, I want to emphasize that I am in no way opposed to social-movement politics. I have been active in some movements. I am suggesting, however, that there is a problem with a rhetorical cycle that seems to reward an uncompromising, absolutist approach to public life, for it results in as much political disengagement as political mobilization. I am searching for a type of politics that is inclusive and open, even to one's ideological opponents.

I pointed out above that the politicians who campaigned on a strident culture-wars theme were not particularly successful in electoral politics. Though cultural warriors won some primaries, and on occasion a seat in the House of Representatives, at the national and institutional level they lost—and generally they continue to lose. Elections have provided culture-wars campaigns with a platform, but have denied them power. The institution of the two-party electoral system has historically fostered compromise, moderation and stability. Therefore, as counterintuitive as it sounds, I think a way to make the political system healthier is to strengthen political parties. . . .

I am not claiming that there is necessarily a "strong center" in American life. Rather, I am recognizing that American political institutions cannot, and are not intended to, represent all the opinions of all Americans. They are designed to marginalize uncompromising minorities. By forcing public positions into the center, and by forcing compromise in the formulation of policy, the institutions of American politics have diffused and defused the passion necessary for war.

Even more important from my perspective is that parties offer avenues to political involvement for ordinary people. People who cannot donate large sums of money or who do not have access to the media can still volunteer time and energy to a party. They meet others with similar interests and values (and others who are not so similar) and are rewarded for their loyalty, diligence and energy. . . .

SUSTAINING A DEMOCRATIC POLITICS

Two other factors important to sustaining a democratic politics need to be mentioned. First is strong voluntary associations, such as churches and civic groups, that bring people together around broad common agendas rather than narrow special interests. Despite laments over their decline, such groups remain an important force in American life—indeed, the recent attention devoted to their so-called decline may actually help their vitality as it emphasizes their importance.

Second is an increasingly constructive media. The reliance on media-centered political strategies has seemed to exacerbate the culture-wars cycle. But there is some evidence that media are beginning to move away from the conflict-obsessed, personality focused, photo-op and sound bite–centered stories that are used so effectively by candidates such as Buchanan. There have been serious discussions suggesting that the media donate time for candidate messages and that those messages be issue-oriented rather than attack ads. This could help take some of the demand for media money out of the political system. . . .

Many culture-wars analysts suggest that American politics displays the inevitable division between two groups who have fundamentally different worldviews. We have seen that this is a great exaggeration. While culture influences our politics, no culture war dominates them. Nor is the culture war the sole cause of the public incivility and political stagnation that often seem to show up on the evening news.

Rather, the culture war is a style of rhetoric that is useful for political activism in a media age. This style has become more noticeable since the institutions that used to mobilize people for political involvement have become attenuated. Revitalized political parties could undermine the media stranglehold on our political language and provide more avenues for the nonwealthy to get involved in politics.

The style of politics bemoaned by those worried about culture wars will no doubt always be with us. But that style is not all-encompassing. While the culture-wars idea does reflect the demands of certain activists, it is not the only game in town. Indeed, the tendency of American political institutions to produce centrist political solutions is probably usefully offset by the cultural tendency of movement-style politics to inflate ideological differences into "war." Institutional pressures are centripetal – they force things into the center. Ideological tendencies are centrifugal—they push politics to the margins. This may be a complementary relation. Institutions stagnate without social movements' pressures to change. And if we are weary of a politics that seems to reward the unreasonable—that seems like a culture war—the answer may well be in revitalized institutions that can moderate it.

| "There can be no doubt that a lot of fundamentalists are deeply involved in the organizations of the Right."

CHRISTIAN FUNDAMENTALISM PROVOKES CULTURAL CONFLICT

Virginia Ramey Mollenkott

Christian fundamentalists, who claim to interpret the Bible and the history of Christianity as literal fact, constitute much of the membership of right-wing organizations, argues Virginia Ramey Mollenkott in the following viewpoint. These organizations typically claim to be defenders of morality and traditional values, Mollenkott points out; however, she maintains, they often promote racist, anti-Semitic, antifeminist, and antihomosexual agendas. Mollenkott teaches English and women's studies at William Paterson College in New Jersey. She is also a contributing editor of the *Witness*, a monthly Episcopalian journal.

As you read, consider the following questions:

1. What example does Mollenkott provide to support her view that the fundamentalist interpretation of the Bible is not truly literal?
2. In which right-wing organizations are Christian fundamentalists deeply involved, according to the author?
3. What is the hidden political agenda of the proposed religious equality amendment, in Mollenkott's opinion?

Reprinted, by permission, from Virginia Ramey Mollenkott, "A Time to Bear Witness," *The Witness*, October 1996.

Fundamentalism as a world view only really began as a movement in the 1920s. The term was coined in 1921 by Curtis Lee Laws, a Baptist, to identify someone who stood for what Laws called "the historic doctrines of the Christian faith"—as opposed to modern religious liberalism.

The conservative Inter-Varsity publication, the New Dictionary of Theology, defines a fundamentalist in several ways: 1) an evangelical Protestant (that's not accurate as far as I'm concerned); 2) an anti-modernist, meaning somebody who subscribes to the traditional, supernaturalistic beliefs of biblical Christianity; and 3) someone militant in this anti-modernism and militant in anti-secularism. So most recently what has been under fire from fundamentalists like Pat Robertson has been the Supreme Court's ban on prayer in public schools, any tendency to liberalize laws or attitudes towards homosexuality and any tendencies toward equal partnership between women and men in church and society. This latter part is especially focused on taking away women's reproductive freedom.

WHAT IS FUNDAMENTALISM?

Historically—that is, since the 1920s—fundamentalism has been the term to refer to those who hold the "five fundamentals" of the supposedly historic Christian faith: the miracles of Jesus taken literally; the virgin birth of Jesus taken literally; the substitutionary atonement of Jesus (which was not important to the church until Anselm developed the idea in the early 12th century); the bodily resurrection of Jesus; and the word-for-word inspiration of the Bible.

Even before fundamentalism had the name, two California oil millionaires, Lyman and Calvin Stewart, had begun to spread the movement by funding 12 booklets called The Fundamentals. Between 1910 and 1915 they mailed these to more than three million pastors and other Protestant Christian leaders. The booklets denied Darwinian evolution, attacked the higher criticism of the Bible and affirmed the Mosaic authorship of the Pentateuch. They also affirmed the five fundamentals. The rest of the booklets took issue with Roman Catholicism, socialism, atheism, Mormonism—and, above all, they took issue with naturalism. So, for instance, anybody who would explain Jesus' walking on water by suggesting that maybe there was a sandbar would be accused of gross unbelief.

But as somebody who came out of the fundamentalist camp, I want to say that the literalism is exceedingly selective. I'll just give one illustration: the Hebrew prophet, Joel, who said that

God's spirit speaks and says "I will pour out my spirit upon all flesh and your sons and your daughters will prophesy and also upon the servants and upon the handmaids, in those days will I pour out my spirit" (Joel 2:28). Fundamentalists accept the Book of Joel as part of the verbally inspired scriptures, but they don't take Joel's words literally; in fact they do not believe that God's spirit could be poured out on all flesh. Because if God's spirit could be poured out on all people, it would include Mormons! It would include feminist theologians! It would include Muslims, Jews and atheists.

SURPRISING STATISTICS

The fundamentalist movement is so decentralized that it's very hard to pin down. For instance, many journalists or critics of fundamentalism assume that the term is synonymous with the Religious Right and you will very frequently hear it used that way. Some see the Religious Right as a reincarnation of Jerry Falwell's now defunct Moral Majority. Some see the Religious Right as a continuance of the conservative political campaigns of Pat Robertson and Patrick Buchanan, and others see it as a kind of broadbased, socially conservative, inter-religious, inter-racial coalition.

I think the truth lies somewhere in the middle of these definitions. A Gallup poll taken at the end of 1994 for the Princeton Religious Center came up with some very interesting statistics, such as that only 18 percent, at that time, of American people identified themselves as members of the Religious Right. I would think that the shift to the Right in this country would make it slightly larger now. Seventy-four percent were able at that time categorically to deny that they are members of the Religious Right. And then there were about 8 percent that weren't sure whether they were in the Religious Right or not.

Of those who identify most strongly with the Religious Right, 21 percent are women, 23 percent are college graduates, 26 percent are Southern people, 30 percent are African Americans, 16 percent are Democrats and 24 percent are Republicans. Only one person in three who claims to have been "born again," also considers himself or herself a member of the Religious Right. I should remind you that during the 1992 presidential election all the Republican and Democratic presidential and vice-presidential candidates identified as "born again," which right away should warn us not to make too easy an equation between born again-ism and the Religious Right.

It's not correct loosely to identify the Religious Right with fundamentalism. Is it accurate to relate it with Republicanism? Clearly not, although it's important to note that the Religious Right currently is very influential in the Republican Party and certainly several organizations are actively trying to take over the GOP. Fifteen percent of the people who identify with the Religious Right call themselves ideologically "liberal." Another 14 percent call themselves "moderate."

RIGHT-WING ORGANIZATIONS

Despite these complexities, there can be no doubt that a lot of fundamentalists are deeply involved in the organizations of the Right. And I would like to note now some of the organizations and talk a little bit about their agendas.

Accuracy in Academia and *Accuracy in the Media* are two watchdog groups. They fight what is called "liberal bias." According to these groups, we college professors are terrible—we are, they say, trying to rob all young people of their faith.

Then there are the "big three." First, *The Christian Coalition,* founded by Pat Robertson. . . . It is developing greater political sophistication as it attempts to infiltrate school boards all over the country. It claims to be non-partisan, but the IRS is seeking to take away its tax-exempt status because of its political maneuvering. The goal of the Christian Coalition is to put 10 trained workers in each of the nation's 175,000 precincts. As of 1995, they had almost two million members and more than 100,000 precinct leaders in place.

Another of the big three is *Concerned Women for America,* which is the nation's largest conservative Christian women's organization. It supports male headship in the home and in the church. The group's focus is, of course, on anti-feminism. They promote themselves as the conservative alternative to the National Organization for Women. The male corollary is *Promise Keepers,* which is sweeping the country.

The other member of the big three is *Focus on the Family,* led by James Dobson out of Denver. It seeks to defend traditional "family values," but it doesn't seem to know or care that there are at least 40 different forms of family described or implied in the Bible, including equal partnership marriages, commuter marriages, single-parent families, communes and so forth.

FROM ANTI-ERA TO GAY EXECUTIONS

The Eagle Forum, led by Phyllis Schlafly, almost single-handedly defeated the Equal Rights Amendment (ERA) and is still around. *Exodus International* is an organization that claims to have converted thousands of gay men and lesbians to heterosexuality. *Family Life Ministries*, led by Tim LaHaye, seeks to save America from secular humanism. LaHaye, of course, was formerly a Moral Majority leader. *The National Right to Life Committee* opposes abortion and women's reproductive freedom. *Rockford Institute* in Illinois opposes the erosion of traditional values resulting from an increasingly pluralistic society, so it sees multiculturalism as the enemy. *The Traditional Values Coalition* is active in anti-homosexual legislation and opposes even school-based counselling programs for gay and lesbian teenagers. *Scriptures for America is* really out there on the Right. It's a racist, anti-semitic group. It espouses Christian identity theology, which claims that Anglo-Saxons are the Bible's true chosen people and Jews are interlopers! They also believe gay people should be executed.

INCREASED POLITICAL SAVVY

In 1994, Ralph Reed, [then] head of the Christian Coalition, released what he calls a "contract with the American family." Among other things, this contract called for a tax credit of $500 for each child and the right of homemakers to contribute up to $2,000 annually toward a tax-sheltered annuity. These are initiatives intended to help the middle-class American family, initiatives I liked. But what's especially interesting to me is that the contract does not frontally attack homosexuals, even though that group has raised a lot of its money by anti-homosexual rhetoric. It also takes a fairly centrist position about abortion and moves away from suggesting compulsory prayer in the public schools.

These modifications from the usual fundamentalist positions indicate a growing political awareness that the American people will tolerate only so much forcing of views onto other people. Don Browning, who is a professor at the Divinity School of the University of Chicago, was so impressed by this document that he argued in *The Christian Century* that mainline churchpeople ought to discuss it seriously and think about throwing their votes toward it as a way of keeping America from moving even farther to the Right. This is the way liberals are getting co-opted.

Ironically, it is the militia movement that has pushed many Americans back a little bit more toward the Left, especially since the 1995 Oklahoma bombing. I watched with fascination one night as David Koresh went on and on about his understanding of the Bible—the most amazing composite of biblical literalism and his own mad read on himself. It was astonishing! And of course the Weavers of Ruby Ridge also hold a view of biblical inerrancy. The militia movement sees itself as the last line of defense against a government that is hellbent on taking away all traces of opposition to its own policies. There's a great deal of racism and anti-semitism involved: They argue that the "Zionist Occupation government" is taking over America and that argument seems to be gaining ground among many people. It seems meager right now, with about 10,000 members, but it has to be closely monitored because it is so full of violent enmity.

BEWARE OF THE INNOCUOUS

So where do we go from here?

Several lines of action are essential for people such as ourselves. If we want to preserve America's civil liberties and historic church-state division, we'd better keep ourselves well informed. Furthermore, we better learn to read very carefully, because Religious Right literature is getting more and more sophisticated and often sounds exceedingly innocuous.

Here's an example: Lou Sheldon of the Traditional Values Coalition has been pushing a religious equality amendment to the Constitution. The first section reads: "Neither the United States, nor any state, shall abridge the freedom of any person or group, including students in public schools, to engage in prayer or other religious expression in circumstances in which expression of a non-religious character would be permitted, nor deny benefits or otherwise discriminate against any person or group on account of the religious character of their speech, ideas, motivation or identity."

This sounds like the good old American freedom of religion. But in point of fact there are a couple of very glaring problems in it. For one thing, it's redundant. We already have the establishment clause in the first amendment, which protects the rights of minorities and dissidents by placing certain matters like religion outside the reach of transient majorities.

But secondly, to guarantee freedom to engage in prayer or other religious expression wherever expressions of a nonreligious character would be permitted would allow teachers to proselytize students in their classrooms. It would allow students to disrupt class sessions with their religious convictions. It would allow judges to proselytize in their courtrooms. The other hidden political agenda is that the clause forbidding denial of benefits is in there to force taxpayers to pay for vouchers for attendance at religious schools.

We have to be aware that the current primary strategy of the Religious Right is, as I said earlier, to infiltrate school boards, because these positions influence education and therefore eventually could provide a *cadré* of political candidates in the future who have been governed by this particular perspective.

Well, what's the best way to try to transform that strategy? If you've got any energy, run for the school board yourself. But also be there for the debates and when you hear the deceptive rhetoric, expose it. Many Americans are voting for these candidates without having the vaguest idea that they are Religious Right candidates.

BiLL iNteRPRetS tHe BiBLe fOR HiMSeLf, aNd fiNdS it ReMaRKaBLY coMPatiBLe WitH HiS OWN coNVictioNS.

Reprinted by permission of Kirk Anderson.

We must remember that the bulk of Religious Right activists are committed to the use of conventional politics. We can be grateful for that. They are not committed to the use of bombs and guns to get what they want. The best obstacle to that is our own political activity.

We also need to oppose the racism and anti-semitism that is

sometimes expressed by the Religious Right, not by everybody, but by enough people to make us nervous. I think of Tim La-Haye's comment that by rejecting Jesus, Jews brought God's curse on themselves and on Palestine, and Pat Robertson's heavy reliance on well-known anti-semitic literature.

Some of us have lived through the holocaust and we have seen what happened there and it was very largely traceable to Christian theology. So we can't sit still and let this happen again, be quiescent or apathetic about it. Pat Robertson complained, for instance, that "cosmopolitan, liberal, secular Jews are involved in the ongoing attempt to undermine the public strength of Christianity." And he has made similar charges against Islamic leaders.

INTERPRETING SCRIPTURE IN A HEALTHY WAY

Above all I think we have to work in our local congregations and secular communities to teach people a liberating and inclusive way of interpreting the Bible. The Religious Right scores points with the American people by playing on their ignorance of Scripture. That's a vacuum into which they can pour all the interpretations that are the most patriarchal. I think it is vital that we don't lose the battle for the American mind by sheer default because we are too lazy to learn how to read Scripture in a more liberating way. When we're sufficiently outspoken about the radical insights of Scripture, we can help move society in a more healthy direction.

Why have the churches not taught a liberating interpretation of Scripture? I have a feeling that many of the mainline churches are so embarrassed about what happened in the 19th century with slavery, when some leaders defended slavery from a scriptural base, that they don't want to talk Bible study anymore. But if we aren't willing to study a liberating hermeneutic, by default we leave other people to tell the American people what the Bible says. So we could teach through discussions, public forums, neighborly conversations, letters to the editors of newspapers and magazines, and lots of other ways.

If you can say—"This is what I believe, this is my experience"—that should not be offensive to anybody, because it is not the same as talking for somebody else; it is simply bearing witness by standing in your own truth.

"Secular insularity has had a profoundly negative impact on our common American conversation."

SECULAR CONFUSION PROVOKES CULTURAL CONFLICT

Scott M. Morris

In the following viewpoint, Scott M. Morris contends that America's culture wars stem from the inability of secular (nonreligious) people to comprehend the motivations of people of faith. Those who have grown up with no serious understanding of religious ideas often misinterpret or fail to grasp the words and actions of religious people, he maintains. This confusion is especially evident in the media, Morris points out, which seem incapable of acknowledging that most Americans have religious convictions. Unless this secular misunderstanding and lack of communication are clearly addressed, he concludes, Americans will become increasingly alienated from their common culture. Morris is an associate editor of the *Weekly Standard*, a conservative journal of opinion.

As you read, consider the following questions:

1. According to Morris, how would secularly influenced people interpret the word "sin"?
2. What is "Cultural Disconnect," according to the author?
3. What percentage of Americans believe in God, according to Morris?

Reprinted, by permission, from Scott M. Morris, "Cultural Disconnect," The Weekly Standard, December 18, 1995.

M isunderstanding is afoot in America. People are talking, which is good, but they are not understanding each other, which is bad. There is a significant divide in American culture, a divide between a certain variety of intellectual and, not to put too fine a point on it, the rest of the country. This variety of intellectual stands on his side of the divide, ear cupped and heart full of good intentions, but cannot make sense of what he hears coming from the hinterlands. He looks over, studies the dark terrain, grows confused, draws the wrong conclusions, and generally has a bad time of it—whether he is aware of the fact or not.

The split is not between intellectuals and non-intellectuals—it is not between bookish scholars and virile factory workers, or, for instance, between a yacht-bound William F. Buckley, Jr. and a beer-drinking longshoreman. The divide is between people who have been socialized and educated in a secular culture in a way that has sealed them off from religion, and people who are either religious or at least familiar with the language and motivations of religious people.

THE SECULAR WORLDVIEW

A person of the latter persuasion may be decidedly secular in his take on life, but he will know what it means to believe things are otherwise. The person who is to some extent lost in a secular culture, on the other hand, is not really sure what religious people are up to. Because his life has been conditioned by a secular worldview, all convincing explanations of the mysteries of existence are necessarily secular ones. As an educated person, he may know something about religion, but, for the most part, his knowledge is strictly historical or literary—it is parlor knowledge, brittle and dry as dead men's bones.

If he has been exposed to religious thinking at all, it was in a college course in which he read a few pages of Thomas Aquinas or some stanzas of Dante. He will not believe there is a modern-day Aquinas. He will not think it possible for a contemporary artist to be as devout as Dante. He would never suspect that a scientist in the late 20th century could reverently dabble in theology in the way that Isaac Newton did. He might have been exposed to T.S. Eliot's *Wasteland* but would be shocked to discover his *Christianity and Culture.*

This brand of secularism is noteworthy for its insularity. And in its ignorance of the most enduring tradition in Western culture, such secular insularity has had a profoundly negative impact on our common American conversation. Observe, for instance, what happens when someone utters the word "sin" in mixed company. To secularly tuned ears, the word sin stems from an antiquated religious tradition that retains historical and sociological importance at best. This tradition no longer carries contemporary weight. Its symbols and words are recognizable, but those words and symbols are stripped of original content, dressed up in the latest fashion, and denatured. When someone says, "sin," secularly tuned ears do the best they can and produce, "dysfunction."

But while sins must be prayed about and forgiven, dysfunctions must be refunctionalized. Sins require priests and preachers; dysfunctions require politicians and perhaps psychologists. Thinking that a person is really talking about a dysfunction when she uses the word sin does violence to the meaning of the word sin and to what religious people mean when they use the word sin, but it is not necessarily an act of deliberate intellectual aggression. It may be a sign of confusion. It may reveal a type of parochialism that masquerades as cosmopolitanism.

CULTURAL DISCONNECT

And when the confusion becomes acute, it is difficult to ignore. When someone is bold enough to insist that sin is sin and not anything else, when someone is blunt about it, people conditioned by secular insularity eventually go dumb and stare; their jaws agape, their eyes agoggle, a peculiar dysphasia sets in on them like a terrible hangover. There, in all its attendant ugliness, is a phenomenon that might be called Cultural Disconnect.

Cultural Disconnect may be defined as a phenomenon that occurs when people begin to talk past each other because they have been formed, and informed, by different cultures and are not fully aware of the fact. For long, painful moments, people who have been Culturally Disconnected continue to make points and ripostes in what they take to be a shared language, when, after all, they have ascribed different meanings to words belonging to a common vocabulary.

In recent years, Cultural Disconnect has been occurring more and more frequently between those who suffer from secular insularity and those who do not. It occurs on talk shows, news shows, during the course of debates, in polemics waged by usually crafty and sensible cultural observers, at swank cocktail parties, and even in the academy, a place where, as everyone knows, people take it as imperative to understand one another.

It is not that the number of people who suffer from secular insularity is so great, it is that they are conspicuous: They seem to always be on television. When they are not on television, they are writing books or, at the very least, articles, editorials, and newspaper reports. And because they hold positions of great visibility, their analysis of life creates a mystifying national spectacle in which they portray the convictions that are fundamental and familiar to Americans on the other side of the cultural divide as if they were artifacts from another time and place. In movies, television shows, and news broadcasts, Americans see people who resemble themselves to some extent but are strangely bereft of the convictions that in real life are found to be sustaining. They read columns and articles, they read books, and again, there they are—except, no, on second glance, there they are not.

THE CONFUSION OF THE SECULAR MEDIA

It is as if a nation of body doubles is getting all the attention. People who look like Americans, and for the most part act and think like Americans, are being paraded as the real thing. But the telltale clue is there—the people who are getting the airtime and the print space are not very often religious people, while Americans are, more often than not, religious.

A July 8, 1995, Economist article finds America to be a country that "oozes religion," in fact. The article cites polls which suggest that around 95 percent of Americans believe in God, that four out of five believe in miracles, the afterlife, and the Virgin Birth. Nearly three-quarters of Americans believe in angels. Nine out of ten own a Bible. Twenty-seven percent own more than four copies. "Belief in the devil has risen sharply, to 65 percent in a recent poll," the piece continues. That this is not consistently reflected in the American media is unfortunate and curious and maybe absurd—and points to the phenomenon of Cultural Disconnect.

Some beleaguered believers feel so harassed by the funhouse-mirror treatment they receive in newspapers and on television that they posit the existence of a cabal of God-hating intellectuals, a conspiracy of media-savvy secularists, who are out to deprive the nation of its religious life. But there is no such conspiracy, and the intellectuals, journalists, and media and entertainment producers are far from being savvy. They are, in fact, weirdly confused and disjointed. They are severely handicapped, in terms of their ability to understand America. They have eyes, but they cannot see. They have ears, but they cannot hear. American life appears to them as a bizarre pageant where people succumb to inexplicable motivations. National trends baffle them. The cultural zeitgeist forever eludes them.

Mega-churches sprout up across the country just when religion is supposed to be on the wane. Mainstream Protestant denominations evolve nicely and appeal to principles that even they, mired in their secular vision, can applaud, but what happens? Those denominations begin to lose members, and a more robust, evangelical Protestantism begins to dominate the religious landscape. Racism is said to be the great American plague, and Christian fundamentalism is identified as a backward, crudely religious and racist example of what is going wrong, and yet, the explosive growth of Pentecostal churches, the fastest growing branch of Christianity today, utterly defies this paradigm—Pentecostal churches are typically the most racially integrated in the country.

AN EXAMPLE OF SECULAR MISUNDERSTANDING

There have been attempts to bridge the gap, of course. Most of the major networks have attempted to cover the religious nature of the nation and re-connect with Americans. There have been special reports and special editions, in-depth reporting and long, earnest articles, but they only reveal the Disconnect all the more.

A compelling example of this variety of Cultural Disconnect was provided by a summer 1995 segment of the venerable *MacNeil/Lehrer NewsHour* (now *The NewsHour with Jim Lehrer*), that nightly refiner's fire where corrupt half-thoughts and misstatements, where media-hype tactics and pressures, are burned clean. If the *NewsHour* cannot strike a balanced note, there is something wrong in our culture. And that was what was revealed during the August 21, 1995, broadcast, featuring a misunderstanding concerning the Promise Keepers, the grass-roots religious organization for men founded by Bill McCartney.

McCartney, formerly head football coach at the University of Colorado, formed the Promise Keepers in 1990. While he had been a formidable coach, he was, he explains, a poor father and husband and almost lost his family. He knew his failings were not unique and believed a group that bluntly addressed the nation's problems as spiritual problems, and not economic or even moral problems, would provide an answer for men across the country. McCartney believes the only way that lasting change can come about is for individuals to submit themselves to God. There aren't 12 steps. There is one, and only one—to go God's way, or the wrong way.

Richard Ostling, *Time* magazine's religion editor, served as the narrator of the segment. Before the interviews commenced, footage of Promise Keepers gatherings was shown—men raising their hands, praising God, singing. Following the footage, Marie

Fortune, a domestic violence counselor and minister, and Robert Bly, author of the bestselling men's book *Iron John*, were asked to comment on the Promise Keepers. While Fortune clearly understood what the Promise Keepers were up to—and disagreed with them on explicitly religious grounds—Bly seemed lost. It was not that he disagreed with the Promise Keepers agenda— though he did—it was that he seemed utterly perplexed by it, not to mention alarmed.

Secular Humanism

[Secular] humanism can be defined as the fundamental idea that men and women can begin from themselves without reference to the Bible and, by reasoning outward, derive the standards to judge all matters. For such people, there is no absolute or fixed standard of behavior. They are quite literally autonomous (from the Greek *autos*, self, and *nomos*, law), a law unto themselves. There are no rights given by God. There are no standards that cannot be eroded or replaced by what seems necessary, expedient, or even fashionable at the time. Man is his own authority, "his own god in his own universe."

John W. Whitehead, from *America, Christian or Secular?* Jerry S. Herbert, ed., 1984.

Though Bly was described by Ostling as a "liberal Protestant," it appeared he had never before encountered people who act from religious motives. He suggested that the Promise Keepers had been founded in fear, that it would be bad for America in the long run, that it would ultimately be . . . *a political movement.* "This group of enthusiastic men is bound to go politically toward the Christian right wing. There's no other place it can go in American culture. . . . Pat Robertson is waiting."

McCartney put it this way: "We have no political agenda. We have no candidates to endorse. We have no policies to suggest. We're strictly after God's heart for what He would do to rescue our nation from this downward spiral of morality and restore Jesus Christ to his rightful position as the head of every home."

But such words, from Bly's perspective, were code words, and he was crafty enough to decode them. He reacted to McCartney's explanations as if they were a child's explanations, just waiting for the author of *Iron John* to come along and peel away the playground rhetoric to expose the naked political truth.

Implicit in Bly's take on the matter is the view that politics, and not anything else, is bedrock. That means that solutions to problems must be political. Thus McCartney, formerly an eminently capable football coach, drops the ball when he diagnoses his own problems and America's problems as the result of sin, for which the only cure is redemption, not political action.

ATTEMPTING TO CROSS THE DIVIDE

To take another example, in the November 1995 issue of the *Atlantic Monthly*, Harvard theologian Harvey Cox wrote a fine article on the religious right in which he attempted, with some success, to cross the divide. While Professor Cox and the men and women he interviewed at Pat Robertson's Regent University did not suffer from Cultural Disconnect, Cox clearly sensed that some *Atlantic Monthly* readers might, and so the article reads like an ethnographer's travel journal, in which the natives' habits and beliefs are explored and then translated into political terms, which is to say, terms his readers will understand. Cox casts himself as the experienced traveler, trying to convince his readers that the natives at Regent University are people too. The professors who teach there hold advanced degrees from respectable universities, he explains. The students are actually quite bright, he allows. Everyone eats, sleeps, and drinks water to stay alive, just like people back home.

Manifesting scholarly prudence, Cox here and there expresses reservations: "I was still not sure whether Regent was a cause or a college or a little of both." (Of course, there are some who are unsure about Harvard for precisely the same reasons.) But in the end, Cox pointedly explains that those who are "enchanted by deconstruction, postmodernism, and secular philosophies" will find it hard "to engage people like the Regent faculty members." In order to do so, he explains, communication will have to proceed at "the theological level."

That communication will not come easily, but it must come. Cultural Disconnect may be amusing when it occurs during the course of a dinner party, but it is massively destructive when it disrupts national debate and fogs a nation's identity. It is not necessary that everyone agree with everyone else about politics and religion, but even the possibility of genuine disagreement implies some degree of understanding. As long as the evening news, and the magazines of opinion, and sitcoms, and feature films, continue to misunderstand the motives and ideas of Americans of faith, they will be responsible for the detachment and suspicion with which Americans increasingly view our common culture.

Periodical Bibliography

The following articles have been selected to supplement the diverse views presented in this chapter. Addresses are provided for periodicals not indexed in the *Readers' Guide to Periodical Literature*, the *Alternative Press Index*, the *Social Sciences Index*, or the *Index to Legal Periodicals and Books*.

David Barsamian	"Politics of the Christian Right," *Z Magazine*, June 1996.
Peter L. Berger	"The Culture of Liberty: An Agenda," *Society*, January/February 1998.
Peter L. Berger	"Democracy and the Religious Right," *Commentary*, January 1997.
David Damrosch	"Is Pablum the Solution?" *Washington Post National Weekly Edition*, February 9, 1998. Available from 1150 15th St. NW, Washington, DC 20071.
Michael Franklin and Marian Hetherly	"How Fundamentalism Affects Society," *Humanist*, September/October 1997.
Stephen Goode	"Secular Faith Fails: God Is King of the Hill," *Insight*, March 31, 1997. Available from 3600 New York Ave. NE, Washington, DC 20002.
Lane Jennings	"The Clash of Civilizations: Finding Ways to Ease Cultural Conflicts," *Futurist*, May/June 1997.
Donald Lazere	"Reciprocal Follies: No Truce in the Culture Wars," *Tikkun*, March/April 1996.
Micaela di Leonardo	"Patterns of Culture Wars," *Nation*, April 8, 1996.
Joe Loconte	"The Battle to Define America Turns Violent," *Christianity Today*, October 25, 1993.
Marvin Mandell	"Canon on the Left," *New Politics*, Summer 1996.
Robin Morgan	"Our Bodies, Our Souls," *Ms.*, September/October 1997.
James M. Penning and Corwin Smidt	"What Coalition?" *Christian Century*, January 15, 1997.
David Wagner	"Elitist Culture, Extreme Reactions," *Insight*, August 12, 1996.
Garry Wills	"There's Nothing Conservative About the Classics Revival," *New York Times Magazine*, February 16, 1997.

CHAPTER 2

Is American Culture in Decline?

CHAPTER PREFACE

Increasing rates of poverty, violent crime, mental illness, substance abuse, and teen suicide are often cited as evidence that Western civilization—American culture in particular—is in decline. According to social analyst Richard Eckersley, "the United States, the pacesetter of the Western world, shows many signs of a society under immense strain, even falling apart. Recent reports and surveys reveal a nation that is confused, divided, and scared." Many observers, for example, bemoan a national crime rate that has tripled since the late 1960s; others voice concerns about heightened racial tensions, family breakdown, and a burgeoning sense of fear, cynicism, and despondency among America's youth. The cause of this malaise, in Eckersley's opinion, is the failure of Western culture to "provide a sense of meaning, belonging, and purpose in our lives, as well as a framework of values." Eckersley and others maintain that unless modern American society develops a clear and consistent moral structure, it will continue to decay.

Some social observers, however, argue that a new and hopeful phenomenon is emerging in American culture. According to research conducted by sociologist Paul Ray, a subset of the U.S. population, a group identified as "Cultural Creatives," has the potential to initiate an American cultural renaissance. Ray contends that Cultural Creatives represent "the appearance of new values and worldviews that were rare before World War II. . . . [The] new subculture includes people who perceive all too clearly the systemic problems of today, all the way from the local level to the national and to the planetary." In comparison to previous cultures, this new group has "higher standards for spirituality, personal development, authenticity, relationships, and toleration for the views of other people," Ray asserts. Many of those who agree with Ray believe that the first two decades of the twenty-first century will be pivotal in America's cultural evolution. If Cultural Creatives assume leadership roles during this crucial time, they maintain, the United States will develop values rooted in a respect for idealism, spiritual transformation, ecological sustainability, and diversity.

Whether American culture is in a state of decline or progress has been hotly contested in the last three decades of the twentieth century. The authors in the following chapter present opposing views on this intriguing subject.

| "We no longer seem to think our
values are worth defending."

AMERICAN CULTURE HAS DECLINED

George Roche

In the following viewpoint, George Roche argues that a break-down in morality has resulted in America's societal and cultural decline. According to Roche, an overemphasis on the differences between people, as well as a widespread lack of honesty, trust, compassion, and self-reliance, has weakened American society. The decrease in stable two-parent families and the loss of traditional religious faith have also damaged American culture, he contends. Roche is the president of Hillsdale College in Hillsdale, Michigan, and the author of *The Fall of the Ivory Tower: Government Funding, Corruption, and the Bankrupting of American Higher Education*.

As you read, consider the following questions:

1. What is political correctness, in the author's opinion?
2. According to Daniel R. Levine, as cited by Roche, what percentage of polled high school juniors and seniors admitted to cheating?
3. In Roche's opinion, what is the root cause of drug abuse, abortion, teen suicide, and crime?

Reprinted, by permission, from George Roche, "Is the U.S. Morally in Trouble?" *USA Today* magazine, January 1997.

I am an inveterate list maker. I love making lists—of tools and gadgets to buy at the hardware store, grocery staples that need restocking, New Year's resolutions—of the little yet vitally important details of living of which I often need to be reminded. Many of the notes I write to myself, especially those on my own shortcomings, begin with the words, "I must remember to. . . ."

WHY AMERICA IS IN TROUBLE

So, it is not surprising that, when I was asked to reflect on our present culture and the general state of American society, my immediate response was to pick up a pen and pad. At the top of the first page, I wrote the heading: "America in the 1990s: Why We Are in So Much Trouble." The following list is the result, a compilation of what the nation has lost:

• *The loss of values.* Values are the building blocks and mortar that keep our entire civilization together. Yet, we no longer seem to think our values are worth defending. "Political correctness" (PC) dominates the academy and the public square. This doctrine holds that all differences in ideas, values, and lifestyles are equally valid and that any attempt to prefer one over the other is an act of prejudice. Moreover, the differences between people— between blacks and whites, men and women, rich and poor, Westerners and non-Westerners—are more important than the qualities and values they share in common. According to PC advocates, questions of race, gender, class, and power are the only real issues that govern human events.

If you think this kind of thinking is confined to college campuses and our intellectual elites, just consider the 1992 Los Angeles riots, the 1995 O.J. Simpson murder trial, or any number of recent events that demonstrate how values have been destroyed by political correctness. Philosopher Jacques Barzun had it right when he said that political correctness does not legislate tolerance; it only organizes hatred.

• *The loss of truth.* PC advocates claim that truth really isn't objective at all; it depends on our point of view. One person's truth is supposed to be just as good (or, more to the point, just as unreliable) as another's. What has been passed off as "truth" are merely the collective prejudices of the dominant ruling class and culture. We must be shown how to "deconstruct" what we think is true.

The only truth that political correctness will admit is that everything—every poem, book, historical event or person, emotion, attitude, belief, and action—must be viewed in a political context as an instrument of exclusion, oppression, or liberation.

• *The loss of moral literacy.* Honor and virtue increasingly are rare commodities. Cheating and lying have become acceptable, especially in school, because children believe that, with few exceptions, "everybody's doing it." Sadly for America, they may be right. In a 1995 *Reader's Digest* article, Daniel R. Levine notes that *Who's Who Among American High School Students* polled more than 3,000 juniors and seniors who were at the top of their class. Seventy-eight percent admitted cheating and 89% indicated that cheating was common at their schools.

In Kansas, Levine adds, a survey of the same number of college students led to almost identical results. Emporia State University psychology professor Stephen F. Davis found that 76% had cheated. He commented: "The numbers alone are disturbing, but even more alarming is the attitude. There's no remorse. For students, cheating is a way of life."

Educators are not only doing a poor job of teaching the three Rs, they are failing to teach children the difference between right and wrong. Observers have characterized this as "a hole in the moral ozone," "moral poverty," or "moral illiteracy."

A CYNICAL AGE

• *The loss of trust.* We live in what may be the most cynical age in history—and the most gullible. Americans are skeptical about many of the things we should believe, while blindly accepting many of the things we should question. On the one hand, we distrust politicians, journalists, and filmmakers because we know that they often have lied to us and deceived us, but, on the other hand, we still look to them as primary sources of information and interpreters of reality.

According to social scientist Francis Fukuyama, author of *Trust: The Social Virtues and the Creation of Prosperity*, we seem to trust our fellow citizens less and less. This "decline of sociability" dramatically weakens our communities, economy, and civil society, which all depend on the "social capital" that is created by shared goodwill, ethical norms, and expectations. He warns that, if we do not revive our trust in others. we will end up cooperating only under a system of coercion and regulation.

• *The loss of empathy.* I am not talking about what Pres. Bill Clinton meant when he said to the nation, "I feel your pain." By empathy, I am referring to the ability to transcend our own immediate concerns to understand other human beings—to see the world from their perspectives without surrendering our own. Former National Endowment for the Humanities chairman Lynne V. Cheney tells of an incident that occurred in 1994 that provides "a chilling vision of life" without empathy:

"That summer, Mohammed Jaberipour, 49, was working a route in south Philadelphia in a Mister Softee ice cream truck when a 16-year-old tried to extort money. Jaberipour refused, and the youth shot him. As the father of three lay dying, neighborhood teenagers laughed and mocked his agony in a rap song they composed on the spot: 'They killed Mr. Softee.'

"'It wasn't human,' another ice cream truck driver, a friend of Jaberipour who came on the scene shortly after the shooting, told the Philadelphia *Daily News*. 'People were laughing and asking me for ice cream. I was crying. . . . They were acting as though a cat had died, not a human being.'"

Cheney quotes the conclusion of newspaper columnist Bob Greene: "We have increasingly become a nation of citizens who watch anything and everything as if it is all a show." She adds, "But however it has come about, people who laugh at a dying man have no sense that a stranger can suffer as they do."

A Confused and Divided Nation

The United States, the pacesetter of the Western world, shows many signs of a society under immense strain, even falling apart. Recent reports and surveys reveal a nation that is confused, divided, and scared. America is said to be suffering its worst crisis of confidence in 30 years and to be coming unglued culturally—the once-successful ethnic melting pot that the United States represented now coagulating into a lumpy mix of minorities and other groups who share few if any common values and beliefs. Most Americans, one survey found, no longer know right from wrong, and most believe there are no national heroes.

Richard Eckersley, *Futurist*, November/December 1993.

• *The loss of independence and confidence.* I don't know the statistics, but I am willing to bet that there are more laws and regulations on the books than there are people living in the U.S. The state dictates how we should educate our children, earn our living, guard our health, take care of our communities, and even worship our God. Although there has been a tremendous resurgence of conservatism in this country, too many of us still look to Washington to provide a vast array of services that better would be left to the private sector and to assume responsibilities we once proudly bore.

The fact is that we no longer are independent because we have lost confidence in ourselves. We have grown accustomed to thinking that there are some problems that are just so big and complex that only something else that is big and complex—like government—can tackle them.

AN EXPLODED BOMB

• *The loss of family.* The good news is that the vital role of the traditional family at long last is the subject of national attention. The breakdown of the family—rather than poverty, race, or any other factor cited by the liberal establishment—is widely recognized now as the real root cause of rising rates of substance abuse, teen suicide, abortion, academic failure, welfare dependency, and violent crime.

The bad news, though, is that this time bomb isn't ticking—it already has exploded, and we are experiencing the fallout. Nearly one-third of all children are now born to single mothers. If this trend continues, in 20 years, nearly half of all children in our nation will be born out of wedlock. Meanwhile, the national crime rate has tripled in the space of 30 years, and observers like Princeton University sociologist John J. DiIulio, Jr., warn that we are breeding a whole new group of "superpredators"—youths who commit violent acts with absolutely no sense of remorse or respect for human life and who, according to one prosecutor, "kill or maim on impulse, without any intelligible motive."

It is no wonder that, for the first time in decades, almost all the experts on the right and the left in psychology, sociology, social work, and law enforcement agree: Our children need capable, responsible parents who have made a lifelong commitment to each other within the specific institution of marriage. This is because children need stability and consistency in their lives. They need the thousands of little moral and practical lessons that are taught in the context of daily family life. Above all, they need the love that only a mother and father can give.

DISTANCE FROM GOD

• *The loss of faith.* Although millions of us still attend church and profess to believe in a Creator, we hold ourselves aloof from God. He is not, as He should be, the most important, guiding force in our daily lives. In one way, this is more shocking than if we had become atheists. While atheists deny God and His authority, we accept Him, but refuse to take Him seriously. At school, work, social gatherings, and in public, we are too afraid, reluctant, or embarrassed to even mention His name.

We constantly are searching for substitutes just as dieters

crave fat-free cookies and ice cream. We want the taste of faith, but not the substance, and we expect to find it in the trendy new Life Experience Enrichment movement that peddles its secrets at New Age retreats, on motivational cassettes, and in glitzy paperbacks and infomercials.

In terms of sheer numbers, the Judeo-Christian community still is the largest group of any kind in America, but we have embraced a mainly post-Judeo-Christian culture in which traditional forms of any religion are relegated to the "back of the bus."

ALL IS NOT LOST

Yet, after examining this gloomy list, I feel that, despite our troubles, we have many reasons to expect a bright future. There literally are millions of us who, for the most part, do defend our values; tell the truth; live honorably and virtuously; live up to high moral standards; exhibit trust, independence, and empathy; build strong families; and are courageous witnesses to faith.

For more than 200 years, we have found ways of overcoming adversity and succeeding against all odds. Though they may sometimes be threatened, our best qualities—optimism, resilience, moral indignation, ingenuity, charity, compassion, and spiritual strength—have a way of resurfacing when we need them most.

"*[America]* has demonstrated an
astonishing capacity to integrate new
immigrants, to defuse religious, class,
and ethnic hostilities, and to promote
a homogenized national culture."

AMERICAN CULTURE IS NOT IN DECLINE

Charles Lindholm and John A. Hall

Many commentators have recently argued that America is in decline due to a loss of shared moral values and because various
groups are unable to bridge socioeconomic and cultural differences. Charles Lindholm and John A. Hall contest this opinion in
the following viewpoint. For the most part, the authors maintain, Americans emphasize equality, fairness, tolerance, and cooperation in the public arena. Lindholm and Hall contend,
moreover, that most conflicts between classes, ethnic communities, and religious groups are held in check by a stable economy,
a belief in social order, and the tendency of Americans to trust
each other as individuals. Lindholm is a professor in the anthro-
pology department and the University Professors Program at
Boston University. Hall is a sociology professor at McGill University in Montreal, Canada.

As you read, consider the following questions:

1. According to Lindholm and Hall, in what way is the claim
   that Americans do not share a common culture an essentially
   American sentiment?
2. In what ways does the American school system train students
   to be tolerant and cooperative, in the authors' opinion?
3. According to the authors, for what reasons do Americans join
   civic and social organizations?

Reprinted from Charles Lindholm and John Hall, "Is the United States Falling Apart?"
Daedalus: Journal of the American Academy of Arts and Sciences, Spring 1997, vol. 126, no. 2, *Human
Diversity,* by permission of *Daedalus.*

A host of best-sellers have appeared in recent years complaining that the social fabric of the United States is unraveling. What is at issue is not solely the insistent demands emanating from previously unheard-of entities, such as the "Queer Nation" and the "Nation of Islam," as well as from more familiar ethnic and religious groups. Rather, the "new groupism" rests on sophisticated philosophical attacks against the very notion of a common American culture. One such criticism argues that the American dream had content but that this content was so biased and limited, Waspish and racist, that there is no reason to lend it any credence. Another view sees Anglo-Saxon culture in general and American culture in particular as lacking in content, being so individualist and atomist as to deny the way in which collectivities create compelling moral identities for their members. Noting the difference between these two views—one seeks to abolish any common frame and the other seeks to create one—should not obscure their shared belief that the promise of the seal of the United States (E pluribus unum) has now lost its relevance in an atmosphere of "culture war."

RECONSIDERING THE CONDITION OF THE UNITED STATES

The debate about the immorality or absence of a common American cultural value system has been posed in another way by theorists who lament the supposed development of a new American character type, so lacking in moral fiber and fearful of social opprobrium as to have no capacity to make ethical commitments. This is the "other-directed" American made famous by David Riesman and his associates. Following in Riesman's footsteps, Habits of the Heart, the hugely successful portrait of American life drawn by Robert Bellah and his colleagues, presents Americans as individualists without substance, unable to undertake principled communal action because they are terrified to differ from others in a competitive, fluid, and atomistic social world. The claim of diminished social responsibility has also been made from a somewhat different perspective by Robert Putnam, in noting that Americans now "bowl alone"; he sees this development as representing a waning of the social capital hitherto created by the associations of civil society.

A paradox is apparent amidst this plethora of discordant warnings: Americans are imagined simultaneously to be unable to resist the tyranny of groups and to be isolated individualists. This suggests the need for a reconsideration of the condition of the United States in order to reveal the underlying institutional patterns and shared cultural values of the society, and then deciding whether these institutional structures and cultural commonalities are enough to hold America together. . . .

AMERICA'S COMMON CULTURE

Americans generally believe, as one of our students proudly put it, that "we Americans do not have a culture; we are all different." American intellectuals have tended to accept the premise that Americans indeed lack a culture; they assert that the United States coheres because of its institutions and the democratic and liberal ideals that underlie them. So long as Americans have faith in the Constitution and the Bill of Rights, they have no need of a shared cultural identity and can exist within a pluralistic "nation of nations." But this view ignores two important facts. First, to have any lasting effect ideals cannot be institutionally imposed but must resonate with preexistent shared perceptions and ways of being in the world. Many societies, after all, have wonderfully democratic and liberal constitutions yet manage to be totalitarian and genocidal despite them. Second, grade-school civic lessons aside, very few native-born Americans have any clear idea of what the sacred documents of the nation actually contain. They are Americans all the same, instantly recognizable not by their differences but by their enormous similarities.

This commonness of the culture of the United States can be approached by a moment's reflection on the claim noted, namely, that Americans are different and so do not share a culture. No sentiment could be more quintessentially American, for the assertion itself rests on a culturally specific faith that all persons are independent actors, each separately responsible for his or her own fate and endowed with a God-given potential for free choice and agency. Ideally, all such persons are equal before God and the law, with equivalent rights and privileges, and all are worthy of respect regardless of wealth, prestige, or power. This pervasive belief—derived in part from the historical absence of an aristocracy in the United States, in part from the culturally dominant Protestant faith in the capacity of individuals to choose their own fates, and in part from the great social mobility of American society—has always been expressed in ordinary interaction through an absence of deference and by strong moral demands for the expression of equal esteem for all members of the community. The historian David Fischer notes that from colonial times "extreme inequalities of material condition were joined to an intense concern for equality of esteem" as rich and poor "wore similar clothing and addressed each other by first names. They worked, ate, laughed, played and fought together on a footing of equality."

Despite ever greater distinctions in rank and wealth, Americans remain extremely careful to cloak authority relations with the trappings of equality. On the job, subordinates are "team members" whose "consent" and "cooperation" are "requested" by their "supervisor." At home it is perfectly acceptable to have servants or to go to an elite school but not to put the servants in livery or to have a genteel accent; in short, it is politically correct to be rich and powerful just so long as one does not make claims to be different and better. The surest way to be ostracized by Americans is to have the reputation of being a snob; the surest way to be accepted is to be friendly and "nice" to everyone, regardless of status.

THE COMPLEXITY OF AMERICAN MORALITY

American morality is quite complex, particularly because of paradoxes within our culture that permit pernicious and beneficial social phenomena to arise simultaneously from the same basic value. That is, American individualism is something of a double-edged sword: it fosters a high sense of personal responsibility, independent initiative and voluntarism, even as it encourages self-serving behavior, atomism, and a disregard for communal goods. More specifically, American individualism threatens traditional forms of community morality, and thus has historically promoted particularly virulent strains of social problems. At the same time, it represents a tremendous moral asset, encouraging the self-reflection necessary for responsible judgment and fostering the strength of voluntary communal and civic bonds.

Jeffrey W. Hayes and Seymour Martin Lipset, *Responsive Community*, Winter 1993–1994

Such effacement might seem to conflict with the well-publicized self-assertiveness of Americans—an assertiveness strikingly indicated by national surveys showing that 70 percent of Americans think they are above average in terms of leadership. But we should note as well that even more striking statistics apply to Americans' beliefs in their "ability to get along well with others": none think they are below average, 60 percent report themselves to be in the top 10 percentile, and 25 percent say they are in the top 1 percentile. These seemingly contradictory findings can be reconciled once we note that Americans find status and respect primarily through being liked, and they want leaders whom they can like in turn. Therefore, for Americans the ordinary Joe is the better leader, and it makes sense that the majority of Americans, ordinary Joes (and Janes) who try hard to be nice and adapt to the needs of others, feel that they are, as a result, potential leaders.

Americans' "niceness" and distaste for elitism, so often commented on with various degrees of amusement or condescension by foreign visitors, correlates with a fluid social world where there are no clear status markers; this unstable and potentially threatening universe is made liveable by the expectation that one's own friendliness and helpfulness will usually be reciprocated. Such an attitude can only exist in conjunction with a basic sense of trust in the public sphere, which is believed to be populated by men and women who, like oneself, are basically fair, decent, and kind. Social trust is a legacy of the original Protestant covenanted community, now transformed into the larger secularized social world where the primary values are being "well liked" and "getting along well with others." Training toward these ends is clearest in the American school system, where popular students are elected as student body leaders who "represent" their fellow students, where "school spirit" is heavily promoted, and where children are graded on the quality of their "citizenship." Students are also expected to participate in extracurricular activities that oblige them to cooperate together on a voluntary basis. Team sports especially are highly valued as an expression of school spirit and local pride, where individuals can show off their personal talents while helping their teammates to victory through disciplined self-sacrifice and cooperation. These institutions have nothing to do with formal education and everything to do with learning how to participate peacefully in a competitive society of coequal individuals.

MORAL MINIMALISM

Alongside diffuse trust is another characteristic American stance, that of "moral minimalism," which prohibits overt interference with or judgment upon other people. This ethical position of benign detachment, like the requirement to be nice to everyone, is a product of the underlying American value system of individualistic egalitarianism, which means that all persons have the freedom to make their own fates, without restraint from their neighbors, and, concomitantly, should not interfere with anyone else's actions. This American pattern fits well with the roomy and fluid world of the suburb, where there is no need for individuals to confront one another, where it is even possible for members of the same household to have separate rooms, separate schedules, separate meals, and almost no contact. Americans thus tolerate diversity so long as they are not obliged to interact with others who are too different from themselves or with people who are intrusive and make demands on their time and autonomy. . . .

A UNIQUE SOCIETY

America is a unique society based upon shared values of egalitarian individualism and capitalist free enterprise. It has demonstrated an astonishing capacity to integrate new immigrants, to defuse religious, class, and ethnic hostilities, and to promote a homogenized national culture. This culture is animated by dreams of monetary success in the competitive marketplace but is softened by an ethic of generalized social trust and a pervasive interactive style that combines "niceness" with moral minimalism. Within this shared frame of reference, Americans imagine their social universe to be, in its ideal form, an extended family, based on the love and voluntary cooperation of coequals engaged in the joint task of building a community. From the point of view of its citizens, the United States is the best of all possible worlds—one that, by and large, delivers on its promises. Instead of ethnic nationalism, Americans have the nationalism of an ideal: they firmly believe that, if they could, everyone in the world would love to join them and become citizens of the United States.

AMERICA'S INNER TENSIONS

The American experience is fraught, like any other, with inner tensions that provide the dynamic for its movement. What is perhaps unique is that Americans believe that this should not be so. Pervasive idealism about politics, for instance, means that the electorate is continually disappointed when its leaders prove to be fraudulent in their claims that they serve neither themselves nor any interest group, that instead they are dedicated to the higher communal end of representing "all the people." An increased scrutiny of public figures and the widely reported mass contempt for them reflects deep ambivalence toward the political realm, as sacred ideals of selfless community service are increasingly seen to clash with unacceptable realities of difference and interest, and as politicians are revealed to be heroes with feet of clay—something that could never happen if they were not thought of as heroes in the first place.

Another element in the widespread sense of malaise in America is the equally ambivalent relationship Americans have with groups. Alexis de Tocqueville was perhaps the first to note that Americans are great joiners, finding refuge from a competitive universe by associating together in a vast array of civic and social organizations. Important recent research shows that this continues to be the case. There may be truth to Putnam's claim that membership of bowling leagues has fallen, but there is none to his more general notion of "declining social capital"—as can be seen in the huge growth of membership in therapy groups, children's football leagues, and health clubs.

But what matters more than sheer numbers are the beliefs entertained about group life. Outside of the pragmatic sphere of business, associations are believed to be held together, as noted, less by interest than by shared love and mutual caring. Disagreement is kept to a minimum in favor of enjoying one another's company, and there is usually a concerted effort to avoid the appearance of any form of hierarchy, for fear of being called a snob. Each such group feels itself to be unique, though for an outsider the actual differences between groups may appear negligible. For instance, self-identified members of ethnic groups often believe their group has many distinctive rituals, whereas in truth the rituals are shared by almost all Americans. Similarly, middle-class black and white college students may vehemently claim that they belong to completely different "cultures," but for an observer the discernible differences between the two groups are negligible. While we do not seek to downplay the subjective importance of multiple cultural identities in America, there remains everything to be said for Tocqueville's notion that the characteristic American elaboration of small differences is best understood as an effort to establish a personal identity and a place of comfort and community within the competitive world of the United States.

A number of consequences follow from this effort. Members of American groups tend to feel themselves united by shared caring and kind intentions; they are good people and good citizens, acting as "everybody" should act. But they are suspicious of the motivations of members of other groups, who may only be pretending to be decent and caring persons in order to further their special interests against the interests of the whole. For example, college students typically describe their own group as a bunch of friends, while other groups are "cliques." Similarly, American social activists see themselves as trying to draw people into the community, while their opponents describe them as power-hungry and exclusionary.

The tension between an idealized "us" and a demonized "them" manifests itself at every level of American culture. Survey research on the leading members of a variety of influence blocs—labor leaders, businessmen, feminists, bankers, farmers, media people, blacks, students, and so on—shows that in general their ideals are the same as the ideals of the public at large. But they disagree about who *actually* does have influence, and, according to Sidney Verba and Gary Orren, they see "themselves as the victims not of a system deaf to all groups but of a system that 'plays favorites.'" Only one's own group is pure, and only one's own group therefore actually holds the general will at heart. It follows that one's own group should dominate, since only one's own group actually expresses the true voice of the public. This circle of self-delusion and self-congratulation among groups validates public qualms about corruption and degeneration in the political realm, leading to further cynicism about—and withdrawal from—political action and thus a return to the realm of personal friends and family. It should be emphasized, however, that the pervasive ambivalence of Americans about politicians and groups does not threaten the society with disruption. In fact, it makes it harder for any group or individual to present themselves as the savior of the American way, and so provides a base for the mundane continuance of a social order based on trust of other Americans as individuals but distrust of them in groups or as leaders.

Much more troubling is the continued prevalence of anti-black racism in America. While white ethnics (and, to a lesser extent, Asians and Latinos) have been "melted" into American society, retaining only a symbolic cultural identity, those of African descent, who have been in America from its inception, are still excluded and discriminated against despite their best efforts to participate in the American dream. . . .

Black Americans' belief that they can and should struggle against oppression and for justice and equity actually shows the depth of their Americanness. That many white Americans can understand and sympathize with the plight of African-Americans shows that racial prejudice, although generated by the contradictions of American egalitarianism, is never wholly legitimated within it and that the struggle against racism is as much a part of the American grain as is racism itself. . . .

AMERICA IS NOT FALLING APART

In this viewpoint, we have sought to refute the claim that America is falling apart. On the one hand, the institutional structure of the United States has the capacity to diffuse potentially divisive conflicts between classes, religious sects, and ethnic communities throughout society—rather than concentrating them against the state. On the other hand, as long as the economy is healthy, putative new identities and groups do not offer any real challenge to the basic premises of American culture, nor is the highly flexible social fabric of America likely to be torn asunder by their demands. Whether black or white, gay or straight, female or male, the vast majority of Americans continue to believe in the possibilities of economic success and to act as if the world was made up of nice, nonjudgmental individuals, who build familial communities through mutual and voluntary cooperation. Despite the inevitable and wrenching tensions and paradoxes implicit in this idealized belief system, it shows no signs of losing its hold.

| "The revolution that was meant to solve every problem became the problem."

THE 1960S DAMAGED AMERICAN CULTURE

Cal Thomas

Cal Thomas is a nationally syndicated columnist and the author of *The Things That Matter Most*. In the following viewpoint, Thomas argues that the social and countercultural movements of the 1960s damaged American culture. The excesses of that decade— including the anti-authority rebelliousness, sexual permissiveness, drug use, and rejection of the traditional family and conventional religion—produced a society lacking in values and moral fiber, the author asserts. Because of the upheavals of the 1960s, Thomas maintains, America must now contend with fragmented families, increased poverty and crime, poor educational and artistic standards, and widespread alienation and hopelessness.

As you read, consider the following questions:

1. According to Thomas, how much has the American government spent on its war on poverty?
2. What percentage of children born in 1988 will live with both parents until age eighteen, according to the author?
3. According to Thomas, for which project did the National Endowment for the Arts authorize twenty thousand dollars?

Reprinted, by permission of *Imprimis*, the monthly journal of Hillsdale College, from Cal Thomas, "The Sixties Are Dead: Long Live the Nineties," *Imprimis*, January 1995.

I f you slept through the sixties, you woke to a different America. It was the pivotal point of the recent past—an authentic decade of decision. It marked the beginning of a passionate social debate that still divides us. It changed ancient attitudes on matters both public and private. One sixties' radical with second thoughts, Peter Collier, has written, "The stones we threw into the waters of our world in those days caused ripples that continue to lap on our shores today—for better, and more often, for worse." No generation of Americans has ever heard more extravagant promises. Promises of revolution. Promises of utopia. Promises of ecstasy. Promises of justice. Here is a brief look at some of the other features of the sixties' ambitious agenda:

1. *The promise to end poverty.* In 1962, President John F. Kennedy asked Congress for the creation of a "public welfare program" designed to "attack dependency, juvenile delinquency, family breakdown, illegitimacy, ill health, and disability." During the Great Society, these goals were expanded even further, and President Lyndon B. Johnson assured his fellow Americans, "The final conquest of poverty is within our grasp." This massive government effort led one wag to comment, "God is dead but fifty-thousand social workers have risen to take His place."

2. *The promise of liberation from the traditional family.* In the 1960s, Betty Friedan mocked the life of a mother and homemaker as consisting of "comfortable, empty, purposeless days" lacking any possibility for a woman to "grow and realize one's full potential." Children and marriage were represented as the sworn enemy of self-fulfillment. Distrust and suspicion were returned by the young: "Don't trust anyone over thirty" were the passwords for entry into the counter-culture. Jim Morrison, lead singer for the brash new musical group the "Doors," influenced millions of young fans by always referring to his parents as "dead" even though they were still alive.

FREEDOM AND ENLIGHTENMENT?

3. *The promise of sexual freedom.* In 1966, Masters and Johnson cast the blinding light of research into the "dark corners" of human sexuality. Everything was measured, categorized, and revealed. Most Americans were surprised to learn what went on in suburban bedrooms—and kitchens and closets. The lesson drawn? It was less than profound: "Do your own thing." Meanwhile, the infamous Weathermen pursued their "smash monogamy" campaign. Many committed couples were harangued until they admitted their "political errors" and split apart. Marriage began to replace cohabitation as the unpardonable sin. The youth culture

began to experiment with group sex and homosexuality out of a sense of political obligation, as well as a yearning to be trendy.

4. *The promise of "pharmaceutical enlightenment."* Harvard University Professor Timothy Leary urged students in the *Psychedelic Reader* to "Tune in, turn on, drop out" as a surefire method to expand their mental horizons. Happiness and drug use became synonymous. And, of course, flouting the law and convention on the issue of drugs soon led to a general disrespect for all law and convention.

5. *The promise of progressive education.* On the sixties-style open campus, students were delighted to find more and more courses without assignments, lectures, or grades. Universities began to abandon their most basic mission of providing liberal arts undergraduate education. As sociologist Robert Nisbet explains, "The ideologies which gained entry into the academy in the sixties claimed that the fundamental intellectual principles of Western culture were illegitimate and must be overthrown. With that destroyed, terms like truth, good, evil, and soul could be discarded."

6. *The promise of unrestrained expression.* "Little Richard's First Law of Youth Culture," named after a then-popular singer, set the agenda: Please kids by shocking their parents. Beyond popular culture, even "high culture" led by prestigious artistic figures threw off all convention in an effort to redefine the medium and in so doing opened the floodgates of nihilism and perversion in the name of "art."

7. *The promise of God's death.* Radical activists and even once-conventional theologians sponsored an escape from traditional religion and morality in an attempt to create "new values" for a new generation. Some merely wanted to make the church seem "hip" and relevant; some desired to tear it down. Few demurred at all when Chicago Seven defendant and militant atheist Abbie Hoffman proclaimed, "God is dead, and we did it for the kids."

BROKEN PROMISES

The attack on authority was frontal and heavy. Jim Morrison spoke for many when he said, "I have always been attracted to ideas that were about revolt against authority. . . . I am interested in anything about revolt, disorder, chaos—especially activity that seems to have no meaning. It seems to me to be the road to freedom."

The mottoes of the time, charged with wild-eyed, unwashed intensity, tell the story of the sixties: "If you see something slipping, push." "Burn baby, burn." Ideas like personal honor, gentlemanly conduct, loyalty, duty, obligation, and the sacred were all disowned. The past was demolished, like a decaying, outdated historical landmark, to make way for a chrome and glass future.

The decade of the sixties was judged, in its own time, by the height of its aspirations. Today, it can be judged by the depth of its influence. When the evidence is weighed, the verdict is irrefutable: We have lived through the unfolding history of its utter failure. Promises and illusions were shattered like glass. Americans are left to walk carefully among the jagged shards.

To fight poverty, the government has spent beyond the wildest dreams of avarice—let alone Franklin Roosevelt, John F. Kennedy, or Lyndon B. Johnson. For over three decades, we have conducted the greatest social experiment the world has ever seen with $3.5 trillion in government funds. Yet poverty is still on the increase, deeply rooted as it is in fragmented families, and welfare is still a trap that eventually destroys the soul.

THE RESULTS OF "LIBERATION"

Feminist disdain for the family and the sexual revolution have given millions of women the chance to realize their full potential—of abandonment and poverty, that is—and has "liberated" countless children from the affection and care of their parents. The results for children are particularly disturbing, because their suffering has been uninvited and undeserved. The Census Bureau estimates, for example, that only 39 percent of children born in 1988 will live with both parents until their 18th birthday.

Other surveys suggest that over 40 percent of all American children have no set goals, a limited education, and a sense of hopelessness about their lives. It is no wonder that psychologist Judith Wallerstein concludes that almost the same number enter "adulthood as worried, underachieving and sometimes angry young men and women." The doctrine of the dispensable two-parent family—so central to the sixties—turned out to be a lie. Those who embraced it have much to answer for; they have sacrificed too many children on the altar of their ideology.

IMPOVERISHED EDUCATION

Progressive education, designed to provide enlightenment, has generally left students entirely in the dark. At Vermont's Middlebury College, it is possible to take a class called "Popular Culture, Eroticism, Aesthetics, Voyeurism, and Misogyny in the Films of Brigitte Bardot." "Music Video 454," taught at California State University, uses the Rolling Stone Book of Rock Video as its only textbook and places students as extras in rock videos—for credit.

Is it any wonder that stories about the ignorance of college students have become clichés? Recently, a Harvard senior thanked his history professor for explaining World War I, saying, "I never knew why people kept talking about a *second* world war."

THE PRICE OF THE 1960S

The Baby Boomers got most of the cultural redefinitions they wanted, and today liberated America turns out to be a place where it is not very safe to walk down the street, nor very serene to grow up, and not very secure to be married. We are freer to use drugs, to abandon our families, to have sex of any kind, to abort unwanted children. This has undoubtedly left some individuals happier than they would otherwise have been. In some cases it may have prevented other horrible outcomes. But at a serious price: the loss of the first thing people seek from organized society—not economic gain, but rather a stable order in which individuals can make a living, find their interests, worship their God, live their personal lives and contribute to their communities.

This cultural disorder, far more than a mostly imaginary economic disorder, is what gnaws at American minds and threatens our goals today.

Michael Barone, *San Diego Union-Tribune*, July 28, 1996.

Those who once were keepers of the gateways of learning have little left to offer. Their fields have been impoverished by critical theories that reinterpret all knowledge in terms of political and economic power and exploitation. Since the sixties, college professors have taken up political causes as a profession, using the classroom to denounce falsehood and injustice while teaching that truth and justice are illusions. J. Allen Smith, the father of many modern education reforms, confessed: "The trouble with us reformers is that we have made reform a crusade against all standards. Well, we have smashed them all, and now neither we nor anyone else has anything left."

THE HATRED OF BEAUTY

In regard to culture, theories that hate beauty and order have undermined meaning, value, and conscience. Whether it is popular culture or high culture, they have led to ever stranger sins and more startling obscenities. Each year requires more baroque perversions to provoke society's jaded capacity for outrage. The National Endowment for the Arts, official arbiter of the avant garde, illustrates the change. In 1989, the NEA denied a modest request from the New York Academy of Art to provide young painters with skills in drawing the human figure. Susan Lubowsky, director

73

of the NEA's visual arts program, explained, "Teaching students to draw the human figure is revisionist . . . and stifles creativity."

Recently, the distinguished sculptor Frederick Hart, who created "Three Soldiers" at the Vietnam War Memorial, applied for a grant to do a series of sculptures. To his surprise, the endowment turned him down. "The NEA," he said, "told me I was not doing art." Yet the NEA paid $70,000 to fund a show featuring Shawn Eichman's "Alchemy Cabinet," displaying a jar with the fetal remains from the "artist's" own abortion. Around the same time, it authorized $20,000 for a project in Lewiston, New York, that was "to create large, sexually explicit props covered with a generous layer of requisitioned Bibles."

ISOLATION AND CONFUSION

On the front line of the drug war, the news is even more grim. Everyone has seen the effect of drugs on the young, who are seldom more than a handshake away from any drug they can afford. The permissive treatment of drugs has spawned a violent subculture of gangs, guns, and random terror. It has squandered lives, talent, and hope in every school and every community.

The escape from religion and the triumph of secularism have left many Americans isolated, confused, and alone. They are disconnected from traditional sources of meaning, value, and love like the family and the church. Sociologists call them "loose individuals" who are free from traditional restraints, obsessed with self-fulfillment, but uncertain of whether anything makes much difference. They are sentenced, in the words of one writer, to "the dark little dungeon of the ego." Novelist George MacDonald once put it another way: "The one principle of hell is, 'I am my own.'"

A CRISIS OF CULTURAL AUTHORITY

The ultimate result is a genuine social crisis—a crisis, if you will, of cultural authority. How can we make any moral judgments? How can we draw dividing lines between sane and insane, noble and base, beautiful and hideous? How can we know anything about living a good life? How can we cry for reform when "form" has no meaning? Peter Collier and another former sixties' radical activist, David Horowitz, conclude, "In the inchoate attack against authority, we have weakened our culture's immune system, making it vulnerable to opportunistic diseases. The origins of metaphorical epidemics of crime and drugs could be traced to the sixties, as could literal ones such as AIDS."

Where does this leave us? The promises of the decade of the

sixties have been broken. Nearly every victory turned out to be a defeat. The revolution that was meant to solve every problem became the problem. If a cultural crimes trial were to be convened today, like the war crime trials of the past, the testimony of the victims would be damning. An abandoned child. An overdosed teenager. A trapped welfare mother. An ignorant student. A victim of venereal disease. Each could ask, "Where was my liberation?"

"More than ever, America is the land of the free."

THE 1960S BENEFITED AMERICAN CULTURE

Terry H. Anderson

The changes wrought during the 1960s benefited American culture, contends Terry H. Anderson in the following viewpoint. Despite the upheavals and the violence of the decade, its various political movements helped to bring about civil rights for women and minorities, Anderson points out. Moreover, he maintains, the events of the 1960s inspired many Americans to challenge the status quo by demanding personal freedom, progressive education, corporate responsibility, and social justice. Anderson concludes that the 1960s made America a more tolerant, diverse, and democratic nation. Anderson is a history professor at Texas A & M University in College Station, Texas. He is also the author of The Movement and the Sixties, *from which the following viewpoint is taken.*

As you read, consider the following questions:
1. Which political legacies of the 1960s were evident at the 1976 Democratic National Convention, according to Anderson?
2. According to Anderson, in what ways did the new left influence the Democratic party?
3. What was the most successful social movement of the 1960s, in the author's opinion?

"Someday we may look back on these times and laugh," wrote activist Jesse Kornbluth in 1968. "And then again, we may not." Whatever the case, the sixties generation certainly would not be able to forget those times. . . .

But . . . how difficult for a baby boomer to let go; how difficult to summarize an era that changed the lives of so many Americans. Writing legacies of any recent era is fraught with peril. Consider this: How different would an evaluation of the movement [1960s activism for progressive social change] be if this viewpoint had been written after the electoral triumphs of Jimmy Carter, or Ronald Reagan, or Bill Clinton? Or consider this: How differently do Americans evaluate the sixties? Conservatives generally loathe the instability of the era, the extreme behavior, the "permissiveness." They might agree with George Will, who in the 1990s bashed away: "Has there ever been such politically barren radicalism as that of the Sixties? . . . The Sixties are dead. Not a moment too soon." Liberals often dislike the excesses and violence but feel that many changes eventually were beneficial to the nation, labeling it a progressive era. College students then and parents now most likely recall a period of excitement, challenges, hopes, disappointments, new values, and they might agree with Todd Gitlin: "Unraveling, rethinking, refusing to take for granted, thinking without limits—that calling was some of what I loved most in the spirit of the Sixties." Minorities might agree with Roger Wilkins, who when asked what he thought of the sixties simply answered, "Wonderful. It was the time that freed my people." Former hippies might chuckle along with Carl Gottlieb—"Anyone who remembers the sixties wasn't there"—or they might wink and say, "Far out."

Whatever one thinks of the sixties, the tumultuous era cracked the cold war culture and the nation experienced a sea change—a significant transformation in politics, society, culture, and foreign policy. . . .

The political legacies of the sixties were apparent to anyone watching the 1976 Democratic National Convention in New York City. African American Congresswoman Barbara Jordan of Houston gave a stirring opening address, and black Mayor Tom Bradley of Los Angeles and Chicano Governor Jerry Apodaca of New Mexico were selected as two co-chairs of the convention. Grace Olivarez, a Chicana feminist from New Mexico, presented the welfare reform plank to the platform. Cesar Chavez delivered the nominating speech for youthful California Governor Jerry Brown, and also from that state was delegate Tom Hayden. The eventual nominee, Governor Jimmy Carter of Georgia, represented the end of Jim Crow [legalized racial segregation]—in the November election both white and black southerners voted for the same candidate for the first time, delivering the presidency to the first man from the Deep South since before the Civil War.

A Continuing Commitment

For many activists—those who come together to reflect on Sixties movements and events, those who continue to embrace the prefigurative democratic vision of the Sixties in their lifestyles and their work, and those who are actively committed to any of the myriad movements that reflect those values—the Sixties experience is part of a continuing path of political commitment and personal growth. In large part, this movement for democracy is grounded on lessons learned through the experiences of the 1960s.

Edward P. Morgan, *The Sixties Experience*, 1991.

That bicentennial year also revealed the impact of the new left, although those activists had been grumbling since the 1968 election that they had failed to bring about a "revolution," a New America. In 1962 they had set a course for the nation in *The Port Huron Statement*, which condemned racial bigotry, anti-Communist paranoia, popular complacency, corporate irresponsibility, and a remote control government and economy controlled by power elites. Those activists failed to interest the majority in long-term efforts to reduce poverty, reform welfare, or curtail the military-industrial complex. Nevertheless, they succeeded in destroying cold war political culture. Americans no longer live in a society that fears change, that suspects dissent. Activists buried McCarthyism. Demonstrations have become routine. Authorities are questioned, scrutinized, and that has changed official behavior. Government offices are open for public inspection, and activists altered police tactics. No longer are protesters beaten. Police are more educated and integrated; they are trained in crowd control, and they work at improving their relations with all in the community. Because of political activists, empowerment is taken for granted.

The new left also influenced the Democratic party. In 1896, William Jennings Bryan co-opted the Populist party platform of 1892 and thus transformed the Democrats into the party of reform. Eighty years later the Democrats did the same, embracing ideas expressed in *The Port Huron Statement*. Since then, they have become the party of civil rights, personal freedom, environmentalism, corporate responsibility, and a foreign policy emphasizing human rights. Moreover, political activists of the 1960s pried open democracy, which earlier reformers had done by extending the vote during the Jacksonian and progressive eras. This time, the movement wrestled political control from white males who for years had been negotiating alone behind closed doors. Activists revived the old progressive idea, You *can* fight city hall, and what activist Bo Burlingham noted in 1976 will remain pertinent for some years: "The convulsions of the last decade have produced something that has fundamentally altered the terms of American politics . . . change is both possible and necessary."

DEMANDING CHANGE

The movement inspired citizens of all types to express their democratic rights, to demand change, and that included conservatives. The backlash began as a response to blacks marching for their civil rights and to students making demands on campus. The struggle raised issues of integration and equal employment opportunity, and that contributed to white flight to the suburbs and charges of "reverse discrimination." Because of race issues, many white working men deserted the party that had boosted and represented them, the Democratic, and became conservatives who voted Republican. The counterculture and women's movement shocked other citizens and they joined the backlash: Phyllis Schlafly and her campaign Stop ERA [Equal Rights Amendment]; Anita Bryant and her crusade against sexual liberation; and a host of others who appeared as televangelists on the *700 Club, Praise the Lord Club,* and *The Old-Time Gospel Hour*—conservatives who reached the zenith of their popularity during the first administration of the "Reagan Revolution."

Ronald Reagan's triumph in 1980 did not overturn the 1960s; there was no return to 1950s America. While the president was very popular, the majority of citizens did not honor his call for traditional social roles or support his environmental views, cold war foreign policy, or attempts to dismantle civil rights legislation and defeat the Equal Rights Amendment.

In fact, sixties political values marched on during the 1980s, and a central theme since has been inclusion. Every primary campaign and convention since has included delegates representing all Americans. Jimmy Carter named more women and minorities to his administration than any previous president, and by 1984 civil rights activist Jesse Jackson had formed his Rainbow Coalition and was running for the Democratic nomination for president. That year female Representative Geraldine Ferraro accepted the party's vice presidential nomination. Republican presidents during the 1980s named Hispanics, African Americans, and women to their Cabinets and to the Supreme Court, and a member of the sixties generation, Bill Clinton, pledged and then appointed a Cabinet that would "look more like America." The long era of white men exclusively controlling the body politic was over.

IMPROVED RACE RELATIONS

America became multicultural—a legacy of the struggle. For minorities, the sixties were a legal and political revolution. In just a few years minorities overturned centuries of legal inferiority and discrimination and obtained their rights guaranteed by the Constitution—an astounding achievement for any society. President Lyndon Johnson proposed and Congress passed the Civil Rights Act of 1964, Voting Rights Act of 1965, Fair Housing Rights Act of 1968. With the support of the Supreme Court, the nation integrated political facilities, ended all voting restrictions, and accepted the idea that men and women charged with a crime should be judged by a jury of their peers. The 1960s killed the legal system called Jim Crow, and since then citizens have witnessed the unprecedented election of people of all races and the rise of minority political power, from mayors and police chiefs of predominately white cities, to governors, Congress, the Cabinet, and the Supreme Court. Furthermore, Black Power advocates stimulated a flourishing of cultural pride that spread to Hispanics, Native Americans, and other ethnic groups, all of whom have embraced empowerment. The federal government answered ethnic demands by ruling against discriminatory practices by businesses and agencies and by enforcing bilingual ballots and education. Ultimately, the struggle challenged Anglo America, and the result was a new definition of "American."

The struggle also diminished stereotyping and racism. That was apparent as early as 1975 when a Cabinet member, Earl Butz, made a racist joke and was forced to resign. Since then, a black leader who was hated by millions, mistrusted by presidents, harassed by the FBI, and assassinated—Martin Luther King, Jr.—has become a national icon. Congress established a federal holiday observing his birthday, placing him on equal footing with Washington, Jefferson, and Lincoln. Numerous opinion polls since have demonstrated that racism as measured by slurs and stereotypes has declined, especially among the young. Compare white racial convictions before and after the 1960s. Attitudes that had been held for centuries have changed considerably, have become more tolerant. Television programs and movies today depicting minorities would not have been possible without the struggle, and school textbooks are more inclusive than at any time in our history. Opinion polls in the 1990s demonstrated that whites and blacks, three to one, felt that race relations have improved since the 1960s and two-thirds felt that the nation has made significant progress. "There's room for improvement," stated black restaurant owner W.A. Mathis in 1994 about race relations in Mississippi, "but it's 99 percent better than it used to be.". . .

THE BENEFITS OF FEMINISM

The establishment today includes more women than ever before—a legacy of the women's movement. At the beginning of the new wave of feminism, editor John Mack Carter of *Ladies' Home Journal* published a statement that raised eyebrows. "The point is: this is 1970. All peoples and both sexes are free to reexamine their roles. They are free to grow where they have been stunted, to move forward where they have been held back, to find dignity and self-fulfillment on their own terms." Radical as it seemed then, the statement now is taken for granted. Since then, a "woman's place" is her decision. On television, gone are the days of June Cleaver. Sitcoms since have portrayed numerous career females, from *Hill Street Blues* to *Murphy Brown*. Heroines can be as complex as heroes. Feminists confronted sexism, provoked men to reconsider their views, and along the way brought about men's liberation. Men have the freedom to choose whether to be the provider, the decision-maker, to stay at home with the children, or to remain single. Roles shifted, as demonstrated by polls in the 1980s that a majority of citizens agreed that men and women should share housework and child-rearing equally. Feminists also changed the family. In the 1950s about 70 percent of families were traditional: a dad who was the breadwinner, and a mom who was the wife, mother, and homemaker. By 1990 only 15 percent of families fit that description. More women than ever before are working, and while the economy was significant in pushing them out of the house and into the office, contemporary opinion polls demonstrate that a majority of females want marriage, children, *and career*. Naturally, that strained the family. Divorce rates have doubled since 1970, but another view is that people no longer feel obligated to spend their entire lives in loveless marriages. "It now appears," pollster

81

Louis Harris noted in 1987, "that the country is witnessing a radical and even revolutionary change in the basic role of women within the family unit." Sex roles have not ended, of course, but because of the movement, America has become a more androgynous society with more flexible views on those roles than at any time, and of any nation.

Activists also were successful in winning legal and political power. Although feminists did not succeed in getting the Equal Rights Amendment ratified, they utilized civil rights acts and decimated discriminatory state and federal laws. During the 1970s most states revised divorce laws, established the idea of common property and no-fault divorce, and accepted the notion that women were full and equal partners in marriage, not subordinate to the husband. Women also revolutionized American politics. While very few had been elected before 1970, by 1990 women had become mayors, governors, congresswomen, senators, and Supreme Court Justices. Two decades after the Strike for Equality, Texas elected a female governor and senator, California elected two such senators, and they had become prime ministers in nations such as Britain, Canada, Norway, Poland, and Turkey. By the time a female becomes president, few will be concerned about the question, "Would you vote for a woman?". . .

A MORE OPEN SOCIETY

The argument here is not that the women's movement brought about complete equality, a condition reserved for utopia. In fact, as feminist scholars note, liberation generally helped white, middle-class women, having much less impact on the poor, and it contributed to the feminization of poverty since new laws made it easier for husbands to abandon their families. The number of single mothers living in poverty has soared. Since liberation, women do more, often receiving the double burdens of home and work, while they listen to the media discuss the so-called burdens of being independent.

Nevertheless, activists exposed private matters long suppressed—abortion, harassment, incest, lesbianism, rape, wife and child beating—forcing public discussion that resulted in a more open society. They challenged the traditional system of education and brought about more sensitivity in the classroom and in textbooks, and they inspired female writers who flooded the nation with new, exciting literature and scholarship. Moreover, in a relatively short time, feminists revolutionized the legal status of women while they changed relations between males and females that had existed for centuries, resulting in more freedom to define their own lives. Because of feminists, women have more opportunities, more equality, more freedom, than at any time. "It changed my life," Betty Friedan simply wrote. The women's movement resulted in changes so profound, and so accepted, that to the ire of many older activists, young females today often take their rights for granted and have to be reminded of their mothers' status. Women's liberation was the most successful social movement of the sixties—and of American history. . . .

RESULTS OF THE COUNTERCULTURE

The counterculture resulted in a value system that has survived with the baby boomers. Surveys by Daniel Yankelovich Group in the early 1970s were confirmed in the late 1980s by Peter Hart Research Associates. The ethics of about 30 million people were altered in a meaningful way by the 1960s events, especially by civil rights struggle, women's liberation, and the war. Some 16 million also stated that personal changes were the result of the counterculture. Those who participated in some aspect of the movement are different from their parents. These sixties people are more skeptical about experts, leaders, politicians, and about institutions—the church, government, and military. They are more flexible, introspective, and tolerant, especially concerning race, living arrangements, and personal behavior. They are more open about their feelings, compassionate, and more liberated sexually. Women feel that they have the same right to sexual satisfaction as men, as demonstrated by a revolution of opinion about premarital sex: The double standard has been buried. Even during the conservative 1980s, numbers soared of interracial marriages, gay and lesbian couples, and single men and women living together. Cohabitation and other alternative living arrangements are common. Being "normal" is no longer a mandate for behavior: Be yourself. Sixties people are more interested in self-fulfillment, defining their own lives, and they often question authority and do their own thing: Let it be.

Most of the counterculture values that since have become clichés still influence behavior. America is more casual in dress and behavior than ever before, and the daily diet includes a wide variety of health foods as corporations proclaim on their packages, "No Artificial Flavors or Preservatives." States have repealed laws prohibiting various forms of sexual behavior between consenting adults, and they have decreased penalties for personal use of drugs. Gone are the days when a court would sentence Timothy Leary to years in prison for half an ounce of marijuana, a drug that still is the most common illegal one in the nation. Youth is not necessarily defined by age, as demonstrated by a legion of middle-aged joggers, hikers, swimmers, rock stars, and others participating in behavior that in the 1950s would not have been appropriate. The result is more personal freedom than at any time in the history of the Republic—so much in fact that youth since has had little to protest, and some have become bewildered with all their options. As James Reston wrote about the graduating class of 1985, there was "nothing to confuse them but freedom." More than ever, America is the land of the free.

"TV executives claim they are just 'reflecting society,' but they are shaping it, as well, helping to mainstream the coarse, confrontational attitudes embedded in gutter talk."

POPULAR CULTURE IS CONTRIBUTING TO AMERICA'S DECLINE

John Leo

American popular culture is contributing to the nation's moral decline, argues nationally syndicated columnist John Leo in the following viewpoint. Television, he points out, is a prime example of such decadence. Its gratuitous sex and violence reflect the nation's moral and cultural depravity, he maintains. Furthermore, he asserts, because television and advertising influence society, ignorance, incivility, and brutality are increasingly permeating American culture.

As you read, consider the following questions:

1. In what way has Chevrolet advertising helped to mainstream aggressive, confrontational attitudes, in Leo's opinion?
2. According to the author, what kind of contradictions pervade today's uncivil society?
3. In Leo's opinion, how could American culture begin to reform itself?

Reprinted, by permission, from John Leo, "Who Is to Blame for the Decline of Culture?" *U.S. News & World Report*, April 24, 1996. Copyright 1996 by U.S. News & World Report.

The cops on the hit television drama *NYPD Blue* have much fouler mouths in the 1996 season. Even the elegant lieutenant, a reserved family man, now uses gutter language. This confuses a successful characterization that has evolved over three years, but the producers don't seem to care. Pushing the envelope is apparently the important thing.

Sometime in 1996, a regular character on *NYPD Blue* used a crude street term for female genitals, apparently a first in broadcast television. The F-word may be the only nasty term left unheard in TV dramas, but that sails out to audiences now and then during post-game football interviews and music award shows.

"There are no gatekeepers left at the networks," says Bob Garfield, columnist at *Advertising Age*. "Aside from the F-word and saying that Advil is better than aspirin, you can get away with anything now."

Television Shapes Society

Does language really matter? TV executives claim they are just "reflecting society," but they are shaping it, as well, helping to mainstream the coarse, confrontational attitudes embedded in gutter talk.

Advertising does it too. Chevrolet has a TV commercial showing a frustrated woman in a Camaro passing a leering trucker. As the voice-over gives us her angry thoughts about her boss, her ex-husband and an incompetent waitress, she thrusts a blurred arm in the air at the loutish driver. The ad agency says she is waving, and at the end, she apparently is. But viewers know what kind of hand signal preceded the wave. General Motors (GM) is celebrating the joys of giving other drivers the finger.

Other TV ads are worse. Among the recent themes are defecation (an ad for a Maryland mall) and oral sex (an excruciatingly gross ad for a little-known hamburger chain).

Nothing makes the declining level of civility more obvious than the fact that large corporations now feel free to cash in on it. Would GM have sponsored a bird-flipping commercial as recently as 1991? Partly because of the highly publicized furor over Calvin Klein's kiddie-porn ads, partly because the anything-goes ethic is now so strong, corporations are more willing to get attention through aggressive, assaultive advertising. They understand that in-your-face messages that shred social norms can move the merchandise by playing to the current sour, anti-social mood. Thus the rapid spread of ads urging us to break all the rules or just make up our own.

Of course, if everyone paid attention to all those narcissistic rule-breaking messages, the result would be total chaos. After all, William Bennett says, "these ads urge individuals to be precisely the kind of people whom nobody would want as an employee, boss, colleague, friend, brother, spouse." As part of the establishment, major corporations don't really want a rule-breaking society, but they are willing to push the message if there is money to be made from it.

AN INCREASINGLY UNCIVIL CULTURE

Years ago, the critic Lionel Trilling wondered what would happen if the adversary culture of artistic elites actually pervaded the whole society. Well, it would look pretty much like what we have now: a culture that celebrates impulse over restraint, notoriety over achievement, rule-breaking over rule-keeping, and any kind of incendiary expression over minimal civility.

NEW THEORY ON WHY DINOSAURS BECAME EXTINCT

McCARTHY/AMARILLO GLOBE-NEWS/CREATORS SYNDICATE

Reprinted by permission of Pat McCarthy.

And a society increasingly drawn to anti-social ideas would inevitably be torn by contradictions: people outraged over anti-women attitudes who can't bring themselves to criticize women-hating rappers, senators who go on the most explosively uncivil radio shows to deplore the loss of civility in politics, the rise of authority figures who don't believe in any kind of authority at all, a culture that mourns social breakdown but keeps celebrating the people who produce it.

Each week seems to bring new benchmarks in incivility. When Commerce Secretary Ron Brown's plane went down, a popular New York talk show host said that as "a pessimist" he feared that Brown might have survived. (Later he apologized.) And in pro basketball, where the level of anger and hostility grows ever higher, another referee was assaulted, knocked across the scorer's table by a Los Angeles Laker who disagreed with his call. Magic Johnson, an icon of a more civil era, said maybe he shouldn't have bothered to come out of retirement.

The largest contradiction may be that a society which badly needs a serious discussion about civility seems determined not to have it. In part, this is because the word "civility" is associated with raised-pinkie gentility and the nannyish hectoring of the young.

And all attempts at reform must come to terms with the '60s generation and its belief that social forms and norms are hypocritical masks for the status quo. Sometimes they are. But our levels of political, social and commercial discourse are now so low that it is surely time to try restoring civility from the bottom up. The alternative would seem to be an increasingly stupid and brutal culture.

A start would be zero tolerance for messages and tactics aimed primarily at degrading and enraging opponents, or cashing in on the fashionable nihilism of the day. This new intolerance should apply equally to angry anti-abortion demonstrators harassing doctors at their homes and angry gay demonstrators attempting to degrade the various symbols and trappings of Christianity. Isn't this a modest proposal?

"*American movies and television,
deservedly subject to much
criticism, are monumental assets.*"

POPULAR CULTURE REVEALS AMERICA'S STRENGTHS

Ben J. Wattenberg

In the following viewpoint, Ben J. Wattenberg contends that important values such as individualism, heroism, and compassion are evident in American popular culture. He concedes that there is too much sex and violence in American movies and television programs; however, he argues, the most popular films and shows are enjoyable and well made and reflect essential American values. Furthermore, he maintains, due to their popularity overseas, American films, music, books, and television could help export the ideals of democracy, liberty, and pluralism abroad. Wattenberg is a senior fellow at the American Enterprise Institute, a conservative think tank. He is also the author of *Values Matter Most*, from which this viewpoint is adapted.

As you read, consider the following questions:

1. According to Sydney Pollack, as cited by Wattenberg, what is a common theme in American movies?
2. What were the top movie hits of the early 1990s, according to the author?
3. In Wattenberg's opinion, why should cultural conservatives avoid blanket condemnation of American popular culture?

Something often is missed in the argument about the state of American culture: Many aspects of our cultural situation are healthy. As I have argued in *Values Matter Most*, political leaders should act boldly and dramatically on social issues. But I am dubious about the idea that we will get much done by slaying fire-breathing cultural dragons. Some of those dragons are friendly critters.

Let us look at pop culture, a big cultural issue. Movies and television make up a large and contentious part of that issue of pop culture. I concede that too much tawdry, violent, promiscuous and evil material is being purveyed. Still, I suggest that American movies and television, deservedly subject to much criticism, are monumental assets.

The distinguished director Sydney Pollack (*Tootsie, Out of Africa, The Firm*) reminds us that American movies, with all their flaws, almost invariably have a common theme. "The hero shapes destiny," he says. Pollack's comment is pretty close to the old American value of individualism. S. Robert Lichter, codirector of the Center for Media and Public Affairs, concurs: "Our studies of television programming have been coded for individualism, but it is so pervasive in American entertainment that we have never even published the material."

DOES TV VIOLENCE CAUSE SOCIETAL VIOLENCE?

Would the incidence of violence, sex and intoxication seriously diminish if those topics disappeared from our screens? That seems to be the apple-pie view of most psychologists (and of Lichter). But it is not a point that has been proved. Indeed, how could such a proposition seriously be validated? In a television-drenched society, just where do the subjects for comparison come from? Social scientists would need two groups similar in home environment, heredity and school environment—except that one control group would have been fed a totally different diet of television fare. Would the violence found in news and cartoons be counted? Does violence on-screen that is punished on-screen reduce or increase the incidence of violence off-screen? Is the violence portrayed rewarded or punished? Is the sex displayed wanton or loving?

Professor Jonathan Freedman of the department of psychology at the University of Toronto reviewed the literature in 1984 and concluded that "there is little convincing evidence that in natural settings viewing television violence causes people to be more aggressive." In 1992, he wrote that "research has not produced the kind of strong, reliable consistent results that we usually require to accept an effect as proved. It may be that watching violent programs causes increased aggressiveness but, from a scientific point of view, this has not been demonstrated. Our public statements should reflect this."

THE POPULARITY OF AMERICAN ENTERTAINMENT

But suppose there was some direct relationship between popular entertainment and the apparent erosion of cultural values. What could we do about it in any public way? We could try to return to censorship. Some conservatives talk wistfully of the good old days of movie censorship. There would be legal hurdles, but not impossible ones.

But do we want broad censorship on sex and violence? And how much good could it do? The answers are no, and not much.

I do not refuse to see movies with naked women in them— realistic ones, arty ones and not-so-arty ones. Nor do scores of millions of other Americans. In the recent past, that number included a lot of good ol'boys and their wives in pickup trucks, watching X-rated movies at the drive-in on Saturday nights and getting home early because, after all, they had to be in church the next morning. These days they may get the same sort of movies in the corner video store.

I do not like much violence in drama. But market tests show lots of Americans do. Shakespeare understood the popular lust for blood and so did Sophocles, in whose plays characters tear each other's eyes out on stage. Cartoon violence, horror shows and cowboy and gangster shoot-em-ups were around long before the current argument started.

Now, Hollywood does not deserve a free pass in this debate. Many Hollywood people make the case that what appears on the screen is only reflecting American reality and it is what Americans want to see. Perhaps. But critic Michael Medved was correct when he said a few years ago that for a long time, Hollywood pretty well ignored a potentially large family audience by concentrating mostly on themes that were violent or sexually driven. (More recently, there has been an abundance of such family fare.)

Not only Americans, but people around the world enthusiastically are embracing our visual pop-culture industry. Today, that industry operates in a climate that is more free than ever, more popular than ever and more global than ever. Incredibly, in Europe, 80 percent of the movie box-office receipts come from American movies. In 1990, 21 of the 25 top movies in Japan were American. Beyond that, American television programs and videocassette tapes are in living rooms around the world. In 1994, for the first time, American companies received more than 50 percent of their theatrical revenues from foreign sources.

WHAT EVERYONE IS WATCHING

And what are people in America and around the world watching? The dozen biggest movie hits released during the 1980s were E. T., *The Return of the Jedi, Batman, The Empire Strikes Back, Ghostbusters*, three *Indiana Jones* movies, *Beverly Hills Cop, Back to the Future, Tootsie* and *Rain Man*. This is not exactly your run-of-the-mill dirty dozen of pornographic violence.

And the same holds true for the early 1990s. Among the top 10 movies in each year from 1990 to 1994 were: *Home Alone, Terminator II, Dances with Wolves, Boyz'N the Hood, Thelma and Louise, Silence of the Lambs, Hook, Beauty and the Beast, Aladdin, A League of Their Own, Dick Tracy, Ghost, Jurassic Park, The Firm, Sleepless in Seattle, In the Line of Fire, Mrs. Doubtfire, Teenage Mutant Ninja Turtles, Naked Gun 2½: The Smell of Fear, Forrest Gump, The Lion King, The Santa Clause, Schindler's List, The Fugitive, True Lies, Lethal Weapon* and *Wayne's World*. Yes, surely there is some violence, sex and stupidity in the list, even, in *Lambs*, some creative cannibalism. Yes, there is some political subtext, and, alas, it rarely is conservative. But mostly these are enjoyable, well-made stories, just like in the good old days. They appear in theaters around the world and then are reaired on television, along with American television dramas and sitcoms, some good, some not.

During the 1994 Moscow summit, President Bill Clinton met with Russian President Boris N. Yeltsin. But Russians, like Americans, were not paying much attention to issues of the North Atlantic Treaty Organization (NATO) or nukes in the Ukraine. Across 11 time zones, Russians were talking about TV's *Twin Peaks*.

THE "SOFT POWER" OF AMERICAN CULTURE

So I offer only certain cautions, applicable across the board but particularly to cultural conservatives. Conservatives, like liberals, can blame America first. Condemning the product too easily may condemn the people who purchase the product. Conservatives may fall victim to the liberal disease: Trash-America exaggeration in the cause of tactical victory. You can hear those old-fashioned elitist wheels spinning: Maybe we need a few government regulations to deal with the problem. Maybe we need a super V-chip so that the government will do what parents ought to do. Why worry?

Because there is a second view of America. You can hear the

retrograde voices around the world: Who are these Americans to tell us how to live? We know best, our people aren't ready for liberty. We know best—liberty brings pornography, liberty brings alcohol, liberty brings crime, liberty brings dependency, liberty breeds separatism. Modern conservatives should not be bolstering that case.

AMERICAN VALUES AND POPULAR CULTURE

There is indeed some violence, sex, and obscenity in American popular culture. But who says that is not part of America? More important, however, generally accepted American values are also at work: upward mobility in *Working Girl*; The fight against the establishment in *Beverly Hills Cop*, *Dirty Harry*, and *Thelma and Louise*; pluralism in *Driving Miss Daisy*, *Jungle Fever*, and *Grand Canyon*; populism in *Rocky*; patriotism in *Top Gun*; technology in *E.T.* and *Back to the Future*; individualism in *Dances with Wolves*, *Home Alone*, and *Tootsie*. It would be exceptionally hard to eliminate American exceptionalism from American entertainment. And it won't happen.

Ben J. Wattenberg, *American Enterprise*, May/June 1992.

Americans care a great deal about telling their story and changing the world. Once this tendency was labeled manifest destiny. At times that harbored racist overtones. We understand now that we can't clone the world American-style. But the American missionary idea lives on. It is as old as John Winthrop's "city on a hill" and as recent as Ronald Reagan.

American movies, television, music, books and magazines have such pervasive worldwide influence that it is asked: Is the world Americanizing? That trend toward Americanization also is driven by immigration, tourism, language, advertising and international commerce. Harvard's Joseph Nye calls it "soft power" and ranks it high. Our foreign policy is moving from Henry Kissinger to Arnold Schwarzenegger.

A MENU OF VIEWS AND VALUES

Is all this good for America? Of course it is, if we think we have something to offer. Is all this good for the world? I think so, but the peoples of the world will have to decide that for themselves. They, and only they, ultimately will decide whether the individualist, democratic, pluralistic and marketplace values offered by the American cultural imperium are of some use as the world reshapes itself in ways we cannot yet foresee. More so than at any other time in history, people have a choice: A menu of views and values is available.

People everywhere want to share the American experience. They want to be heroes shaping their own destiny. They get that idea in part from our visual culture. Trashing American popular culture, putting it in tight quarters surrounded by a V-chip programmed by cackling congressmen, tends to dilute or muzzle that export. A government-rating system will be either a farce or a tragedy.

I believe that democracy American-style, with all its flaws, still is the last, best hope of Earth, as Abraham Lincoln said. But if our flaws aren't fixed, if the flaws get worse, America will cease to be the model of what can be. It will be the model of another thought: that democracy leads up a blind alley.

We are not the only nation with crime or welfare problems. We are not the only nation troubled about the education of our children. We certainly are not the only nation struggling with the problems of pluralism.

But we are the only nation to which everyone else pays attention. If America works fairly well, there will be a model showing that free expression doesn't yield decadence, that pluralism doesn't yield chaos, that there can be order and liberty, that there can be compassion without dependency—all visible and influential on a billion screens around the world.

If we cannot do that, the rest of the world is in for trouble. When they're in trouble, we're in trouble.

| "What started out as 'tolerance' seems to many to have degenerated into lower standards, unfairness and discrimination."

POLITICAL CORRECTNESS THREATENS AMERICAN CULTURE

Martin L. Gross

Political correctness—the promotion of liberal-minded sensitivity concerning race, gender, and cultural issues—has become a destructive movement that suppresses traditional mores and values, argues Martin L. Gross in the following viewpoint. A left-wing cadre of politicians, journalists, lawyers, teachers, and community leaders—the "New Establishment" has taken over the nation's institutions, wreaking havoc throughout society, he maintains. According to Gross, this New Establishment claims, for example, that women and minorities have been victimized in America and therefore deserve preferential treatment in hiring and university admissions. Such preferential treatment is actually a politically correct version of discrimination, a new form of intolerance that is undermining American culture, he contends. Gross is the author of several books, including The End of Sanity: Social and Cultural Madness.

As you read, consider the following questions:

1. According to Gross, why have more than one hundred words been removed from the Scrabble dictionary?
2. Which social programs are rooted in political correctness, according to the author?
3. In Gross's opinion, how has political correctness weakened the armed forces?

"A merica is going crazy!"

The lament is heard from Bangor to Bakersfield as Americans shake their heads about the ludicrous incidents of social and cultural madness that bombard them daily. One after another, people are entertained or frightened, as examples of absolute nonsense replace good sense in a once-pragmatic nation. Reality is being turned upside down, creating a topsy-turvy culture.

America is rapidly experiencing a sociological and philosophical change—almost entirely for the worse, conservatives say—as traditional truths are replaced by false sociological theory. It occurs daily, in many manifestations, yet it escapes understanding.

EXAMPLES OF CULTURAL MADNESS

Some examples:

• At Williams College, a young female student was castigated because she refused to use a school-approved coed bathroom.

• In New York City, a mugger subdued by a police officer sued for use of excessive force and won in court.

• More than 100 words have been deleted from the Scrabble dictionary for fear someone might be offended.

• In almost every medical school, "affirmative-action" females are admitted as future doctors even though they score 14 percent lower on the physical-science admission test than do men, pushing out better-qualified applicants and threatening the future of the profession. Minority medical students score even lower.

• Most students in a bilingual New York college failed to graduate. Why? Because they couldn't pass a simple test in English.

• Parents of a disruptive child who threatened to kill schoolmates sued the school when the child was suspended. They were awarded $20,000 a year for private-school tuition and $360,000 in legal fees.

• At Stanford University, the major course in Western civilization was discontinued because it was too "Eurocentric," as if that is not the basic culture of the nation.

• The U.S. Forest Service in California advertised for only "unqualified" female fire fighters. The reason? A pool of qualified men was blocked by the court to satisfy a gender-equality ruling.

• At Georgetown University, Shakespeare no longer is required study of English majors because officials claim the Bard is not politically correct.

Are these aberrations of normal life accidental and coincidental?

Hardly. They all are interconnected by-products of the "New Establishment," a group of politically correct academics, politicians, judges, lawyers, journalists, bureaucrats, military personnel and foundation leaders who have taken control of virtually every one of the nation's institutions.

Quietly and unseen, unknown and ruthless, they have assumed power from the Old Establishment, promoting a changed vision everywhere. This New Establishment has replaced traditional mores and values with a relativistic "experimental society" that masquerades as "sensitive." Conservatives say it fails citizens of all races and genders and is spawning a new racism and sexism.

What started out as "tolerance" seems to many to have degenerated into lower standards, unfairness and discrimination. It has brought such programs as affirmative action, bilingualism, a mass hysteria of sexual harassment, "multiculturalism" instead of "uniculturalism," political correctness, weak college curriculum, irresponsible court decisions reaching up to the Supreme Court, a dubious coed military, distorted arts and an immigration policy that purposely penalizes Europeans—all within a framework of strict conformity in which fashionability reigns.

SOCIETAL INSANITY

The litany of social and cultural madness continues unabated:

- At Harvard University, grade inflation is so rampant that 84 percent of seniors recently graduated with honors.
- In the Army, among female soldiers returning on a ship from the Persian Gulf War, one in 10 were pregnant.
- In New Jersey, dentists infected with the HIV virus are not required to reveal their ailment despite several nationwide deaths associated with contact between HIV-infected dentists and their patients.
- At the University of Pennsylvania, in a state in which thousands died at Gettysburg to defeat slavery, African-American students are segregated in special dormitories.
- Alice Walton, daughter of Sam and one of the nation's richest women, was granted an affirmative-action bond-dealer contract because she is a woman.
- At several colleges, students in freshman-orientation sessions introduce themselves by saying, "My name is John (or Jane) and I'm gay."

Again, these are not isolated or unconnected incidents. They are part of a burgeoning contemporary gestalt, the result of attitudes developed by the New Establishment that conservatives regard as unraveling the fabric of the nation. Underlying much of it are the concepts of "victimization" and "exploitation," that the New Establishment claims are part and parcel of American civilization—which historians traditionally regarded as one of the fairest in history.

A Nation of Victims?

Developed partially out of discredited Freudian thought, the New Establishment thrives on the theory of "victimization," in which everyone deserves special treatment, except for the "white male." Or is it the "White Whale," the Moby Dick of history? In their lexicon, America is seen as the home of "exploitation." Whites always exploit blacks and hispanics. Men exploit women. Adults exploit children. Teachers exploit students. The judicial system exploits criminals and prisoners. Citizens exploit legal immigrants and everyone exploits the illegals. Even the thin subjugate the fat, the tall the short.

The macabre humor is that the supposedly exploited "minorities," including favored women, now make up some 70 percent of the entire population!

The New Establishment has divided the nation into groups, each of which seeks surcease (even revenge against) the dominant one. It is a clever, destructive scheme that pits one piece against another, all at the expense of the nation. It is a system of social individualization that gnaws at the very basis of a decent society.

What is developing, conservatives worry, is a totalitarian secular theocracy with a dogma that must be obeyed at the risk of professional and personal ostracization, a new McCarthyism of much larger proportions than the prior one. If George Orwell was wrong in predicting 1984 as the year of Big Brother, was he off by only a dozen or so years?

The New Establishment's Agenda

At the core of the new belief is that people—especially women and minorities—fail because of rampant "discrimination." This is a central notion of the New Establishment. The experience of two small, true "minority" groups, American Jews and Asians, refutes this dogma. Together, they account for only 5 percent of the population, but excel in education and the professions far above their numbers. When people are asked why, they often respond: "Because they were discriminated against and had to work harder." But supposedly that same discrimination destroys the will and efficacy of women, blacks, hispanics and other minorities. America can hardly have it both ways.

Top targets of the New Establishment have been the courts

and the executive branch of the federal government, which conservatives say have overextended the rights granted them. The Constitution is clear that all citizens are entitled to "equal protection under the law." If a qualified male is barred from medical or law school and his place is taken by a person of a favored race or gender, the Constitution has been violated.

The Origins of Political Correctness

The term "political correctness" seems to have originated in the early part of the twentieth century, when it was employed by various species of Marxists to describe and enforce conformity to their preferred ideological positions. Books, films, opinions, even historical events were termed politically correct or politically incorrect depending on whether or not they advanced a particular Marxist view. There is no indication that the revolutionary ideologues and activists of that period spoke of political correctness with any trace of irony or self-mockery.

Eventually the term dropped out of the political lexicon, only to be revived in the early 1980s when it came into use by spokesmen for assorted contemporary ideologies: black consciousness and black power, feminism, homosexual rights, and to a lesser degree pacifism, environmentalism, the counterculture in general. The new *Webster's College Dictionary*, published by Random House, defines political correctness as "marked by or adhering to a typically progressive orthodoxy on issues involving especially race, gender, sexual affinity, or ecology." These days, as most people know, the home of such "typically progressive orthodoxy" is the American university.

Dinesh D'Souza, *Commentary*, October 1991.

The Supreme Court has been deficient in recognizing this. In sexual harassment, it has ruled that a woman can sue if the work environment is "hostile" because of pin-up pictures, a Puritan concept in a sex-drenched society. The Equal Employment Opportunity Commission, on its own, has even established the rules of courtship, deciding that "excessive complimenting" of a woman also is harassment.

In the case of affirmative action, the Court of Appeals in Texas has ruled in the 1992 *Hopwood, et al. v State of Texas, et al.* case that race and gender cannot be taken into account for admission to law school, a ruling that protects citizens in only three states. Recently the Supreme Court refused to hear the case, no doubt realizing it finally would be forced to deal with the clear language of the Constitution and rule affirmative action illegal.

In the military, the mixing of sexes has weakened morale and efficiency but is excused on grounds of political correctness. At West Point, women cadets perform less well than men, physically and academically. Physical requirements are lowered for them and the majority of women pursue "soft" majors instead of the traditional and difficult engineering degree sought by men. Class ranking is then skewered by a gender-balanced point system.

The military sexual-harassment epidemic is the reverse side of the fact that fornication is routine in the services, where in new barracks women soldiers occupy rooms next to men. "When we come in for morning inspection, we sometimes find male and female soldiers in bed having sex," a former field commander now at the Pentagon confesses. The punishment? Confinement to barracks! If an illegitimate child results, the Army subsidizes its care and doesn't discipline either of the parents.

This feminization of the services was summed up by a Pentagon-appointed female consultant. The Army, she concluded, is just "too masculine" in its approach.

IMMIGRATION POLICY

Another concern of the New Establishment has been the U.S. immigration policy, in which Europeans, once the major source of immigrants, today take only 13 percent of the slots. The rationale is that Europeans do not want to come here, which is simply false. In the lottery, in which thousands of permanent visas are reserved for nations cut off by the 1965 law that destroyed our traditional policy, 3.5 million Europeans apply each year for admission! But of 70,000 Frenchmen who wanted to emigrate to America, only 3,000 were permitted (mainly through marriage), while more than 100,000 Mexicans legally immigrated in addition to hundreds of thousands of illegals.

The national ethos is being threatened daily by the New Establishment in every walk of life, conservatives say. They think America needs a wake-up call to defeat its onerous motives, which mainly are to take control of U.S. institutions (lost without public approval) and destroy the fabric of the successful, traditional America.

To defeat the New Establishment, say its critics, America must rededicate itself to fairness, the law and the truth.

| "When closely examined, . . . anecdotes [about political correctness] unravel under the strain of exaggeration, deceptive omission of key facts, and occasional outright invention."

THE THREAT OF POLITICAL CORRECTNESS HAS BEEN EXAGGERATED

John K. Wilson

In the following viewpoint, John K. Wilson contends that political correctness—the promotion of liberal ideals and sensitivity to women, minorities, and other groups—has not, as conservatives claim, become a dangerous left-wing movement that threatens America's cultural institutions. According to Wilson, the so-called political correctness movement is actually a myth created by conservatives in an attempt to discredit liberal convictions. To suppress justified complaints about racism and sexism, he argues, conservatives have publicized exaggerated and occasionally false accounts of political correctness occurring on college campuses and throughout society. Wilson is the author of *The Myth of Political Correctness: The Conservative Attack on Higher Education*, from which the following viewpoint is excerpted.

As you read, consider the following questions:
1. What book was Wilson assigned to read most often in college?
2. Blacks make up what percentage of the faculty at the University of Chicago, according to the author?
3. In Wilson's opinion, what kind of double standard exists in articles and books about political correctness?

When I began to hear about political correctness (PC) as a senior at the University of Illinois in 1990, I wondered what I was missing. Where were the radical students intimidating other students and teachers? Where were the tenured radicals indoctrinating me with leftist propaganda? Where *was* political correctness?

I had encountered leftist professors and students, of course, but I had never thought of them as the "thought police" that Newsweek told me were invading college campuses. Most of the leftists I met seemed like nice people, polite and tolerant of other people's views. And the conservative students and professors I'd encountered didn't seem like victims of a new McCarthyism. They had their own monthly newspaper funded by conservative foundations, their own organizations, and their own campus lectures. I don't recall hearing anyone called "racist" or "sexist" or "homophobic," and I certainly never heard anyone (except perhaps the conservatives) use the phrase *politically correct.* I didn't hear many students challenging the "liberal orthodoxy," but then not many of us challenged any orthodoxies. We sat in class and listened to the teachers and read the assignments and wrote the papers and took the tests.

RAMPANT RELATIVISM?

I went to college as the culture wars erupted in 1987, back when "PC" referred only to computers. But in my first week at the University of Illinois, my philosophy professor assigned America's hottest best-seller, Allan Bloom's *The Closing of the American Mind,* which begins: "There is one thing a professor can be absolutely certain of: almost every student entering the university believes, or says he believes, that truth is relative." This assertion surprised me because I'd never heard anyone say that *all* truth is relative. After all, one of the complaints about politically correct people would be that they believed they knew the truth and intimidated those who disagreed with them. In my classes and my discussions with friends, I constantly heard arguments about what was true and what was false. Perhaps what Bloom mistook for relativism was the politeness and tolerance of these arguments. Unlike the 1960s, the campuses of the 1990s are not fiercely divided by passionate debates about war and justice, and students are less likely to hold extreme views, or to occupy campus buildings to express them. But this wasn't relativism; often it was just uncertainty and a healthy skepticism about any dogma. While Bloom's outrageous statements intrigued me, I found it difficult to believe that he really knew what was going on at most colleges.

Unlike most of the people attacking political correctness and higher education, I am a firsthand witness to what has been happening on college campuses during the 1990s. As a student I've taken more than 150 classes from dozens of departments, ranging from economics to philosophy to women's studies, including the first courses on gay and lesbian history ever offered at my institutions. I had both leftist and conservative professors, and I read a broad range of books from the trendy to the traditional. If anyone could judge whether there was such a thing as political correctness, surely I could. I also read a lot of books on my own, especially books about the danger of "tenured radicals" on college campuses. But there were disturbing discrepancies between what I was reading about PC and the reality in front of my eyes.

EXAGGERATED CHARGES

I read that everything was being "deconstructed" and that the Great Books were being discarded in favor of books by foreigners with strange names like Jacques Derrida, Jacques Lacan, Roland Barthes, and Michel Foucault. I read that under the guise of multiculturalism, leftist propaganda was dominating the curriculum. But the book I was assigned most often in college was Plato's *Republic*. I read it in five classes as an undergraduate at the University of Illinois and an equal number of times as a graduate student at the University of Chicago. While I took some unusual classes with progressive teachers and read some things that will never appear on a list of great books, it was almost entirely through my own efforts to find something different. If I did what thousands of other students had done and took only the standard required classes, I would have encountered very little of the multiculturalism that is supposedly taking over higher education.

Shortly after I graduated, the conservative newspaper on campus printed a front-page article claiming that leftist English professors were trying to ban William Shakespeare (along with Christopher Columbus, John Locke, Adam Smith, John Calvin, and Clarence Thomas). Ban Shakespeare? I wondered. That sounded like the PC thought police.

"Who's trying to ban Shakespeare?" asked an English professor at the booth promoting the newspaper.

"Lots of English professors," answered the woman there.

"Who?"

"Professor Cary Nelson. He hasn't had a lot of nice things to say about Shakespeare."

The conservative newspaper had reported that Nelson's mission "is to forever annihilate the traditional literary canon." In response, Nelson wrote in the campus paper: "I have worked to open up the curriculum to more women and minorities, but I have also published on Shakespeare, and like all my colleagues, I support the department's requirement that all English majors take a Shakespeare course. I have never met an English professor anywhere on the planet who wanted to remove Shakespeare from the curriculum."

Reprinted by permission of Kirk Anderson.

When I looked at the English Department's reading lists, I found a dozen classes devoted solely to Shakespeare, and many more that read his plays. No Derrida, no Lacan, no Barthes, no Foucault showed up in the courses. The PC thought police who won't say "a lot of nice things" about Shakespeare suddenly didn't seem quite so ominous.

"Are you politically correct?" asked the cover of *New York* magazine. Readers were told to test themselves: "Do I say 'Indian' instead of 'Native American'? 'Pet' instead of 'Animal Companion'?" I had to confess that sometimes I said "Native American," mostly to avoid confusion with the Indians in south Asia. I didn't know that saying a word could make me a fellow traveler with the thought police. But the "Animal Companion" part puzzled me. By this definition, I wasn't politically correct; in fact, by this definition I'd never met anyone who was politically correct. Do people really say "animal companion" instead of "pet"? Does anyone accuse those who use the word pet of being a "speciesist"? Would anyone take them seriously if they did? I began to suspect that the "political correctness" movement was no more than the product of someone's paranoid imagination. Being asked "Are you politically correct?" is like being asked "Are you in favor of the international conspiracy of Jewish bankers who control the world?" Of course I'm opposed to an international conspiracy of Jewish bankers controlling the world, but I also know that no such conspiracy exists.

AFFIRMATIVE ACTION AND WHITE MALES

One of the charges I often came across in my reading was that affirmative action denies fair treatment to white males. A professor in my undergraduate political science department (whose faculty is mostly white males) wrote that white male Ph.D.s "probably never will get an academic job interview, let alone a job offer." As a future white male Ph.D., this obviously concerned me. Even though I supported affirmative action, I was a little leery about accomplishing the goal of diversity by making myself unemployed.

But when I thought about my own experiences, I wondered who was really receiving these preferences. After receiving a top-notch education in high school, I went to one of the best public universities in the country, with two scholarships to pay my way and the privilege of being admitted to an excellent honors program. Then I was accepted by one of the best graduate schools in the country, offered a prestigious fellowship, and given a federal government fellowship that will pay me $40,000 over four years to get a free education. How many minorities ever get privileges like that?

I certainly don't see lots of minorities being given these special benefits. It's hard to see many minorities at all. At the University of Chicago (where I'm a graduate student), less than 2 percent of the faculty are black and white males are regularly hired. Only 3 percent of the graduate students and 4 percent of the undergraduates are black. Hispanics are less than 2 percent of the faculty, 4 percent of the graduate students, and 4 percent of the undergraduates. Is this the "victim's revolution" that is going to ruin my future career as a professor?

THE "EVILS OF FEMINISM"

But "racial preferences" weren't the only threat to white males mentioned in these conservative critiques. I often read about the evils of feminism. I heard that women's studies classes had been taken over by radical feminists who were silencing dissenters, attacking men, and indoctrinating their students. But my own experience belies these charges of intimidation.

I took several women's studies classes, still searching for these man-hating feminists who are supposedly politicizing education and intimidating students. But all I found were classrooms full of discussions, not politically correct sermons. And I never encountered any classes in other departments that had such a dramatic impact on the lives of the students. I suppose some "politically incorrect" topics were off-limits—we never had a debate about the equality of women—but I saw far more openness there than in most of the other courses I took.

I remember economics classes where the students never argued about economics but instead answered test questions and homework assignments according to the assumptions of a free-market model that even the teachers admitted was inaccurate. I also took large lecture classes in many departments where hundreds of students copied down identical notes (or purchased them from professional note takers) in preparation for the upcoming multiple-choice test. I finished one fill-in-the-ovals final exam in fifteen minutes while proctors patrolled the lecture hall and checked IDs. Curiously, no one called this "indoctrination," even though it was far more oppressive to me than any women's studies class I took.

THE IRONY OF POLITICAL CORRECTNESS

I never saw a conservative student silenced or insulted or punished in any class for expressing politically incorrect ideas. As a columnist for the student newspaper, I never heard of any conservative being prevented from expressing controversial views by the supposedly ubiquitous "speech codes." The idea that leftist students and faculty dominate American colleges and universities seemed like a joke in view of the general apathy on campus.

The most student activism I ever saw came during the Persian Gulf War in 1991, when students marched in protest against (and some in support of) the war. Perhaps the funniest moment occurred during a small antiwar rally held in a park across the street from a fraternity. Some fraternity members tried to drown out the speeches by playing music on their stereos full blast. To my amusement, the songs they played were Bruce Springsteen's "Born in the USA" and Jimi Hendrix's Woodstock rendition of "The Star-Spangled Banner"—these two antiwar songs were the most patriotic music they could find on their CD racks. But strangely, trying to silence an antiwar rally didn't count as political correctness.

A Curious Double Standard

As I began to examine the stories about political correctness, I noticed a curious double standard. Whenever conservatives were criticized or a leftist expressed some extreme idea, the story quickly became another anecdote of political correctness. But when someone on the Left was censored—often with the approval of the same conservatives who complained about the PC police—nobody called it political correctness, and stories of this right-wing intolerance were never mentioned in articles and books on PC totalitarianism. My own experience made me question the existence of the "PC fascism" I had read about. And as I began to study the terrifying tales of leftist McCarthyism, I found that the truth was often the reverse of what the media reported. While some stories about PC are true and deplorable, the scale of censorship is nowhere near what most people think.

What startles me most about the PC scare is that the critics are so uninterested in what is really happening on college campuses. The anecdotes have become more important than the reality. By force of repetition, these anecdotes have been woven into the tale of a "victim's revolution" on campus. When closely examined, however, these anecdotes unravel under the strain of exaggeration, deceptive omission of key facts, and occasional outright invention. What matters to critics is not the truth but the story—the myth of political correctness. Every PC anecdote retells this myth by ritualistic invocation of the image of leftist thought police. The myth of political correctness is a powerful conspiracy theory created by conservatives and the media who have manipulated resentment against leftist radicals into a backlash against the fictional monster of political correctness.

Periodical Bibliography

The following articles have been selected to supplement the diverse views presented in this chapter. Addresses are provided for periodicals not indexed in the *Readers' Guide to Periodical Literature*, the *Alternative Press Index*, the *Social Sciences Index*, or the *Index to Legal Periodicals and Books*.

Richard Eckersley	"The West's Deepening Cultural Crisis," *Futurist*, November/December 1993.
William R. Garrett	"Cultural Revolution and Character Formation," *World & I*, May 1998. Available from 3600 New York Ave. NE, Washington, DC 20002.
Todd Gitlin	"The Demonization of Political Correctness," *Dissent*, Fall 1995.
Samuel P. Huntington	"The Many Faces of the Future," *Utne Reader*, May/June 1997.
Morton A. Kaplan	"The Misbegotten Sixties," *World & I*, May 1998.
Elizabeth Kolbert	"Americans Despair of Popular Culture," *New York Times*, August 20, 1995.
Donald Lazere	"Pulp Fiction as Degenerate Modernism," *Tikkun*, March/April 1995.
Rod MacLeish	"Call to Clean Up Pop Culture Carries Puritanical Baggage," *Christian Science Monitor*, December 10, 1996.
New York Times	"In Praise of the Counterculture," December 11, 1994.
Paul H. Ray	"The Emerging Culture," *American Demographics*, February 1997.
Paul Craig Roberts and Lawrence M. Stratton	"Proliferation of Privilege," *National Review*, November 6, 1995.
Jesse Walker	"How Johnny Cash Restored My Faith in the Healing Powers of Hip," *Liberty*, May 1996. Available from PO Box 1181, Port Townsend, WA 98368.
Wall Street Journal	"A Confusion over Identity," March 20, 1998.

CHAPTER 3

WHAT CULTURAL INFLUENCES BENEFIT SOCIETY?

CHAPTER PREFACE

A disturbing new trend can be seen in today's schools, declares syndicated columnist John Leo in a 1997 *U.S. News & World Report* editorial. "Some students," he contends, "are unwilling to oppose large moral horrors, including human sacrifice, ethnic cleansing, and slavery, because they think that no one has the right to criticize the moral views of another group or culture." Leo cites the example of a college student who personally deplored the Jewish Holocaust but could not admit that genocide was wrong. "Of course I dislike the Nazis," the student explained to his professor, "but who is to say they are morally wrong?" Leo terms this stance "nonjudgmentalism" and argues that it is partly the result of American educators' recent emphasis on multiculturalism. A primary goal of multiculturalism is to foster acceptance of diversity by increasing students' awareness of the histories and traditions of America's many racial and ethnic groups. However, critics maintain, an overemphasis on tolerance of differences can lead students to conclude that all opinions are equally valuable and that no one should judge the moral worth of any culture's beliefs or practices. To avoid such an outcome, Leo suggests that educators search "for a teachable consensus rooted in simple decency and respect."

Many teachers, on the other hand, reject the argument that multiculturalism fosters moral nonjudgmentalism. In fact, they contend, multicultural education often seeks to expose the immorality of the dominant culture's value system by revealing the lies and inaccuracies in many popular and mainstream interpretations of history. For example, these teachers argue, when students discover that the United States acquired land by exterminating Native Americans—a fact not acknowledged in some history books—they learn that minority perspectives and realities have often been excluded from historical studies. Moreover, by purposefully including minority and female viewpoints in the study of history and literature, multiculturalists maintain, teachers can help students broaden their perspectives and, ultimately, make well-informed moral choices.

Educators, activists, politicians, and theologians continue to disagree about which cultural influences strengthen American society. The authors in the following chapter present differing viewpoints on the effects of religion and multiculturalism on the United States.

"If we are to reverse our cultural
decline, we should begin to take God
much more seriously."

BELIEF IN GOD IS NECESSARY FOR A MORAL SOCIETY

John M. Frame

Belief in God is essential for morality, argues John M. Frame in
the following viewpoint. He maintains that basic ethical principles, which are unchanging and absolute, stem from a belief in
a supreme being who has the power to enforce moral standards.
Furthermore, he contends, upholding God-given moral parame-
ters will help to reverse America's cultural decline. Frame is a
professor of Christian apologetics and systematic theology at
Westminster Theological Seminary in Escondido, California.

As you read, consider the following questions:

1. According to Frame, what are relative standards?
2. In the author's opinion, what happens when people claim to
   accept moral principles without believing in God?
3. Why is it impossible to uphold absolute moral principles in
   an impersonal universe, in Frame's opinion?

Reprinted, by permission, from John M. Frame, "Do We Need God to Be Moral?" *Free
Inquiry*, Spring 1996.

If God does not exist, says Fyodor Dostoyevsky's Ivan Karamazov, "everything is permitted." Which is one way of saying that notions of good and evil lose their force when people cease to acknowledge God.

The course of our society suggests he's right: we've grown noticeably more secular over the past thirty years, banning God from public education and the marketplace of ideas, and our culture's moral tone has declined. Is this merely historical coincidence, or is there a profound relationship between ethics and belief in God?

MORAL VALUES AND GOD

Moral values are rather strange. We cannot see them, hear them, or feel them, but we cannot doubt they exist. A witness to a crime sees the criminal and the victim, but what is perhaps most important remains invisible—the moral evil of the act.

Yet evil is unquestionably there, just as moral good is unquestionably present when a traveler stops to help the stranded motorist on a dangerous stretch of highway. Good and bad are unseen but real, much as God is said to be. Does that suggest a close tie between two mysteries, moral values and God?

Before answering that question, let me make a few clarifications:

The highest moral and ethical values are *absolute*. Anyone who thinks it sufficient to have merely relative standards, based on what individuals or groups *feel* is right, won't see a connection between God and morality.

Of course, some rules are relative to situations. In some countries we drive on the right, in others on the left. But relative standards alone simply won't do. Fundamental moral principles—don't murder, don't steal, and so on—must be objective, binding on all, regardless of private opinions or emotions.

If someone robs you, your outrage is not merely a feeling, like feeling hot or feeling sad. Nor is it merely an opinion generally accepted within your society, as if a society of thieves could legitimately have a different opinion. Rather, you recognize that the thief has done something objectively wrong: something that no one should ever do, regardless of how he feels or society thinks.

THE REASON FOR ABSOLUTE PRINCIPLES

A second clarification: If I say that ethics requires God, I do not mean that atheists and agnostics never recognize moral standards. Even the Bible recognizes that they do (Romans 1:32).

Indeed some say they believe in *absolute* principles, though that, of course, is rare. I contend, rather, that an atheist or agnostic is not able to give an adequate *reason* for believing in absolute moral principles. And when people accept moral principles without good reason, they hold to them somewhat more loosely than others who accept them upon a rational basis.

MORALITY REQUIRES BELIEF IN GOD

"Morality is not yet a problem," wrote Friedrich Nietzsche in 1888. But it would become a problem, he predicted, when the people discovered that without religion there is no morality. The "English flatheads" (his sobriquet for liberals like George Eliot and John Stuart Mill) thought it possible to get rid of the Christian God while retaining Christian morality. They did not realize that "when one gives up the Christian faith, one pulls the right to Christian morality out from under one's feet."

A century later, morality definitely is a problem, perhaps the most serious problem of modernity. And foremost among the reasons for this is Nietzsche's own explanation: the death of God and morality.

Gertrude Himmelfarb, *Human Events*, December 1, 1995.

Nor do I wish to suggest that people who believe in God are morally perfect. Scripture tells us that isn't so (1 John 1:8–10). The demons are monotheists (James 2:19), but belief in the one God doesn't improve their morals. Something more is needed to become good, and that, according to the Bible, is a new heart, given by God's grace in Jesus Christ (2 Corinthians 5:17, Ephesians 2:8–10).

GOD AS ENFORCER OF MORALITY

Why then should we believe that morality depends on God?

To say God exists is to say that the world is created and controlled by a *person*, one who thinks, speaks, acts rationally, loves and judges the world. To deny that God exists is to say that the world owes its ultimate origin and direction to *impersonal* objects or forces, such as matter, motion, time, and chance.

But impersonal objects and forces cannot justify ethical obligations. A study of matter, motion, time, and chance will tell you what *is* up to a point, but it will not tell you what you *ought* to do. An impersonal universe imposes no absolute obligations.

But if this is God's world, a personal universe, then we do have reason to believe in absolute moral principles. For one thing, as Immanuel Kant pointed out, we need an omnipotent God to *enforce* moral standards, to make sure that everyone is properly rewarded and punished. Moral standards without moral sanctions don't mean much.

More important, we should consider the very nature of moral obligation. We cannot be obligated to atoms, or gravity, or evolution, or time, or chance; we can be obligated only to persons. Indeed, we typically learn morality from our parents, and we stick to our standards at least partly out of loyalty to those we love. An *absolute* standard, one without exceptions, one that binds everybody, must be based on loyalty to a person great enough to deserve such respect. Only God meets that description.

What other basis for absolute moral standards can there be? It follows that if we are to reverse our cultural decline, we should begin to take God much more seriously, in parenting, education, and public dialogue. We need to hear much more about God in our public life, not less. And we need leaders who know God and are willing to uphold his absolute standards against the fashionable substitutes of our time. I am now giving advice to believers as well as unbelievers. Lukewarm faith, a religious veneer over a secular worldview, will only add to our present ills. But consider the likely results of a return in heart, in reality, to "one nation under God."

"It is possible to have a universal morality without God."

BELIEF IN GOD IS NOT NECESSARY FOR A MORAL SOCIETY

Theodore Schick Jr.

Supporting moral principles does not require belief in God, contends Theodore Schick Jr. in the following viewpoint. Humans can agree on ethical standards without presuming that morality is ordained and enforced by a supreme being, the author argues. He maintains that Americans need a deeper understanding of ethics and values—not more emphasis on religious belief—in addressing today's social and cultural crises. Schick is a philosophy professor at Muhlenberg College in Allentown, Pennsylvania. He is also the coauthor of *How to Think About Weird Things: Critical Thinking for a New Age.*

As you read, consider the following questions:
1. What is the "Divine Command Theory of Ethics," according to the author?
2. According to Schick, why does the philosopher Leibniz reject the Divine Command Theory?
3. For what reason does Schick denounce the notion that the threat of God's punishment makes people act morally?

Reprinted, by permission, from Theodore Schick Jr., "Morality Requires God . . . or Does it?" *Free Inquiry*, Summer 1997.

Although Plato demonstrated the logical independence of God and morality over 2,000 years ago in the *Euthyphro*, the belief that morality requires God remains a widely held moral maxim. In particular, it serves as the basic assumption of the Christian fundamentalist's social theory. Fundamentalists claim that all of society's ills—everything from AIDS to out-of-wedlock pregnancies—are the result of a breakdown in morality and that this breakdown is due to a decline in the belief of God. Although many fundamentalists trace the beginning of this decline to the publication of Charles Darwin's *The Origin of Species* in 1859, others trace it to the Supreme Court's 1963 decision banning prayer in the classroom. In an attempt to neutralize these purported sources of moral decay, fundamentalists across America are seeking to restore belief in God by promoting the teaching of creationism and school prayer.

The belief that morality requires God is not limited to theists, however. Many atheists subscribe to it as well. The existentialist Jean-Paul Sartre, for example, says that "If God is dead, everything is permitted." In other words, if there is no supreme being to lay down the moral law, each individual is free to do as he or she pleases. Without a divine lawgiver, there can be no universal moral law.

THE DIVINE COMMAND THEORY

The view that God creates the moral law is often called the "Divine Command Theory of Ethics." According to this view, what makes an action right is that God wills it to be done. That an agnostic should find this theory suspect is obvious, for, if one doesn't believe in God or if one is unsure which God is the true God, being told that one must do as God commands will not help one solve any moral dilemmas. What is not so obvious is that theists should find this theory suspect, too, for it is inconsistent with a belief in God. The upshot is that both the fundamentalists and the existentialists are mistaken about what morality requires.

To better understand the import of the Divine Command Theory, consider the following tale. It seems that, when Moses came down from the mountain with the tablets containing the Ten Commandments, his followers asked him what they revealed about how they should live their lives. Moses told them, "I have some good news and some bad news."

"Give us the good news first," they said.

"Well, the good news," Moses responded, "is that he kept the number of commandments down to ten."

"Okay, what's the bad news?" they inquired.

"The bad news," Moses replied, "is that he kept the one about adultery in there." The point is that, according to Divine Command Theory, nothing is right or wrong unless God makes it so. Whatever God says goes. So if God had decreed that adultery was permissible, then adultery would be permissible.

Let's take this line of reasoning to its logical conclusion. If the Divine Command Theory were true, then the Ten Commandments could have gone something like this: "Thou shalt kill everyone you dislike. Thou shalt rape every woman you desire. Thou shalt steal everything you covet. Thou shalt torture innocent children in your spare time. . ." The reason that this is possible is that killing, raping, stealing, and torturing were not wrong before God made them so. Since God is free to establish whatever set of moral principles he chooses, he could just as well have chosen this set as any other.

An Arbitrary Lawgiver?

Many would consider this a *reductio ad absurdum* of the Divine Command Theory, for it is absurd to think that such wanton killing, raping, stealing, and torturing could be morally permissible. Moreover, to believe that God could have commanded these things is to destroy whatever grounds one might have for praising or worshiping him. Leibniz, in his *Discourse on Metaphysics*, explains:

> In saying, therefore, that things are not good according to any standard of goodness, but simply by the will of God, it seems to me that one destroys, without realizing it, all the love of God and all his glory; for why praise him for what he has done, if he would be equally praiseworthy in doing the contrary? Where will be his justice and his wisdom if he has only a certain despotic power, if arbitrary will takes the place of reasonableness, and if in accord with the definition of tyrants, justice consists in that which is pleasing to the most powerful? Besides it seems that every act of willing supposes some reason for the willing and this reason, of course, must precede the act.

Leibniz's point is that, if things are neither right nor wrong independently of God's will, then God cannot choose one thing over another *because* it is right. Thus, if he does choose one over another, his choice must be arbitrary. But a being whose decisions are arbitrary is not a being worthy of worship.

The fact that Leibniz rejects the Divine Command Theory is significant, for he is one of the most committed theists in the Western intellectual tradition. He argues at great length that there must be an all-powerful, all-knowing, and all-good God and consequently that this must be the best of all possible worlds, for such a God could create nothing less. Ever since Voltaire lampooned this view in *Candide*, it has been difficult to espouse with a straight face. Nevertheless, what Leibniz demonstrates is that, far from being disrespectful or heretical, the view that morality is independent of God is an eminently sensible and loyal one for a theist to hold.

A CIRCULAR ARGUMENT

To avoid the charge of absurdity, a Divine Command theorist might try to deny that the situation described above is possible. He might argue, for example, that God would never condone such killing, raping, stealing, and torturing, for God is all-good. But to make such a claim is to render the theory vacuous. The Divine Command Theory is a theory of the nature of morality. As such, it tells us what makes something good by offering a definition of morality. But if goodness is a defining attribute of God, then God cannot be used to define goodness, for, in that case, the definition would be circular—the concept being defined would be doing the defining—and such a definition would be uninformative. If being all-good is an essential property of God, then all the Divine Command Theory tells us is that good actions would be willed by a supremely good being. While this is certainly true, it is unenlightening. For it does not tell us

---

MORALITY DOES NOT DEPEND ON FAITH

Plato argued that the chariot of the soul is led by three horses—passion, ambition, and reason—and he thought that the rational person under the control of wisdom could lead a noble life of balance and moderation. The goal is to realize our creative potentialities to the fullest, and this includes our capacity for moral behavior. A good life is achievable by men and women without the need for divinity. It is simply untrue that if one does not believe in God, "anything goes."

So many infamous deeds have been perpetrated in the name of God—the Crusades, the Inquisition, religious-inspired terrorism in Palestine, the carnage . . . among three religious ethnicities in the former Yugoslavia—that it is difficult to blithely maintain that belief in God guarantees morality. It is thus the height of intolerance to insist that only those who accept religious dogma are moral, and that those who do not are wicked.

Paul Kurtz, *Free Inquiry*, Spring 1996.

---

what makes something good and hence does not increase our understanding of the nature of morality.

A Divine Command theorist might try to avoid this circularity by denying that goodness is a defining attribute of God. But this would take him from the frying pan into the fire, for if goodness is not an essential property of God, then there is no guarantee that what he wills will be good. Even if God is all-powerful and all-knowing, it does not follow that he is all-good, for, as the story of Satan is supposed to teach us, one can be powerful and intelligent without being good. Thus the Divine Command Theory faces a dilemma: if goodness is a defining attribute of God, the theory is circular, but if it is not a defining attribute, the theory is false. In either case, the Divine Command Theory cannot be considered a viable theory of morality.

The foregoing considerations indicate that it is unreasonable to believe that an action is right because God wills it to be done. One can plausibly believe that God wills an action to be done because it is right, but to believe this is to believe that the rightness of an action is independent of God. In any event, the view that the moral law requires a divine lawgiver is untenable.

GOD THE ENFORCER?

There are those who maintain, however, that even if God is not required as the author of the moral law, he is nevertheless required as the enforcer of it, for without the threat of divine punishment, people will not act morally. But this position is no more plausible than the Divine Command Theory itself.

In the first place, as an empirical hypothesis about the psychology of human beings, it is questionable. There is no unambiguous evidence that theists are more moral than nontheists. Not only have psychological studies failed to find a significant correlation between frequency of religious worship and moral conduct, but convicted criminals are much more likely to be theists than atheists.

Second, the threat of divine punishment cannot impose a moral obligation, for might does not make right. Threats extort; they do not create a moral duty. Thus, if our only reason for obeying God is the fear of punishment if we do not, then, from a moral point of view, God has no more claim to our allegiance than Hitler or Stalin.

Moreover, since self-interest is not an adequate basis for morality, there is reason to believe that heaven and hell cannot perform the regulative function often attributed to them. Heaven and hell are often construed as the carrot and stick that

God uses to make us toe the line. Heaven is the reward that good people get for being good, and hell is the punishment that bad people get for being bad. But consider this. Good people do good because they want to do good—not because they will personally benefit from it or because someone has forced them to do it. People who do good solely for personal gain or to avoid personal harm are not good people. Someone who saves a drowning child, for example, only because he was offered a reward or was physically threatened does not deserve our praise. Thus, if your only reason for performing good actions is your desire to go to heaven or your fear of going to hell—if all your other-regarding actions are motivated purely by self-interest—then you should go to hell because you are not a good person. An obsessive concern with either heaven or hell should actually lessen one's chances for salvation rather than increase them.

Fundamentalists correctly perceive that universal moral standards are required for the proper functioning of society. But they erroneously believe that God is the only possible source of such standards. Philosophers as diverse as Plato, Immanuel Kant, John Stuart Mill, George Edward Moore, and John Rawls have demonstrated that it is possible to have a universal morality without God. Contrary to what the fundamentalists would have us believe, then, what our society really needs is not more religion but a richer notion of the nature of morality.

"Lincoln and Webster understood
what too many people have
forgotten—the importance of faith
to the public institutions in a
democratic republic."

RELIGIOUS CONSERVATISM SHOULD BE PROMOTED

Ralph Reed

Ralph Reed, the former executive director of the Christian
Coalition, is the president of Century Strategies, a firm that provides campaign consulting services to conservative political candidates. In the following viewpoint, Reed maintains that the
United States has always been a strongly religious country.
Moreover, he contends, most American churchgoers are conservative in outlook and support traditional moral standards. In the
cultural and political arena, however, religious people are often
stereotyped as being intolerant or extremist, Reed states. Rather
than clinging to such stereotypes, he argues, Americans should
welcome and promote the political input of religious conservatives, as they have much to offer to a troubled nation.

As you read, consider the following questions:

1. According to Reed, what percentage of Americans pray daily?
2. In the author's opinion, what sort of value system has been
   promoted by the nation's elites?
3. What incidents does Reed cite as being the consequences of
   the ban on school prayer?

Reprinted, by permission, from Ralph Reed, "Democracy and Religion Are Not
Incompatible," USA Today magazine, July 1997.

Amerinca is a nation unique in the history of the world. It is not the product of an accident or evolution. In spite of its tenuous connection to Great Britain, it is not a natural extension of an empire. America literally is, in the words of 17th-century European explorers, a "New World."

The founders were free to decide its future, and they chose, with conscious purpose, to invent a nation the like of which never had been seen. Thus, America is a nation with no kings, no royalty, and no privileged classes. It is a nation held together by a bond of common experience and a vision of uncommon greatness. America is George Washington's "common country," John Adams' "glorious morning," and Abraham Lincoln's "inestimable jewel."

AMERICA'S SPIRITUAL VISION

It is a nation in which one becomes American not by accident of birth or ethnic heritage, but by subscribing to an idea. No one truly becomes a Frenchman merely by moving to France or a Spaniard simply by moving to Spain. Yet, America has lifted its lamp beside the golden door of entry to immigrants of all races and all countries and bids them welcome to what author Irving Howe called "the good country."

It is not blood or marriage that counts, but a vision of a society based on two fundamental beliefs. The first is that all men, created equal in the eyes of God with certain unalienable rights, are free to pursue the longings of their hearts. The second belief is that the sole purpose of government is to protect those rights.

The first Americans shared this deeply spiritual vision. Most Americans still do. That is why, in the words of a 1995 *U.S. News and World Report* cover story on religion in America, the U.S. is—with the sole exception of Israel—the most devoutly religious nation in the entire world. That is a fact borne out in experience, not just posited in magazine articles. According to public opinion surveys, 92% of Americans believe in God; 83% believe that the Bible is the infallible word of God; and 57% pray daily. Nearly 130,000,000 attend church every Sunday. That means there are more people worshipping God on Sunday morning than are watching "60 Minutes" on Sunday night.

There can be no better testimony to the faith of this nation than the reception that Pope John Paul II received when he visited the U.S. in 1995. Millions of Protestants and Catholics welcomed his message of spiritual renewal. Individuals of every faith and no faith at all watched and listened as this remarkable man of God called on Americans to remember that there is more to life than themselves.

The Pope's message was far from new. It was the same message delivered by the Founding Fathers. The American Revolution, which established a new nation, was not merely inspired by political or economic oppression, but was a revolution of faith, arising from a great spiritual awakening that was sweeping the world in the 18th century. It should come as little surprise, then, to find the affirmation in the Declaration of Independence that there are certain truths which are "self-evident, that all men are created equal, that they are endowed by their Creator with certain unalienable rights." The Founding Fathers were certain that these rights are granted by God, are afforded His protection, and are not to be infringed upon by government.

THE NEED FOR FAITH IN GOD

George Washington, America's first president, wrote, "I am sure there never was a people who had more reason to acknowledge a divine interposition in their affairs, than those of the U.S. I should be pained to believe . . . that they failed to consider the omnipotence of God, who is alone able to protect them."

The nation's second president, John Adams, added, "Our Constitution was designed for a moral and religious people only. It is wholly inadequate for any other." By this, Adams did not mean that the Constitution was meant for people of any specific faith. He opposed religious tests for public office, as do I and most Americans. The point Adams made was far more profound. He meant that, to create a nation where government was small, limited, and confined to enumerated functions, one must have a virtuous citizenry animated by faith in God and moral values.

The nation's founders possessed a view of the world and government that necessarily presupposed a people obedient to an internalized code of conduct—based upon that first, and in my mind still the best, code of law found in the books of Moses—that made a large central government superfluous. It was this view that French statesman Alexis de Tocqueville wrote about in the early 19th century: "The Americans combine the notions of [religion] and liberty so intimately in their minds, that it is impossible to make them conceive of one without the other."

From the Quakers in Pennsylvania to the Congregationalists in New England, the Catholics in Maryland, and the Baptists in Virginia, America is a nation undergirded by faith, built by faith, and enlivened by faith. It is not a faith in word alone, but an active, transforming faith. Look around today and what you will see are the fruits of our national faith. Throughout the U.S.'s history, America's faithful millions have founded orphanages, hospitals, lending libraries, and charities. America's first public schools were founded by clergymen. Its first colleges were divinity schools. Children learned to read by using the Bible as a textbook. McGuffey's Readers, which sold 120,000,000 copies during the 19th century, contained lessons drawn directly from Scripture. Historian David Herbert Donald points out that Abraham Lincoln, one of the most well-read presidents, had just a single year of formal schooling. On the dirt floor of a log cabin, young Lincoln learned how to read by poring over the pages of his mother's Bible. The first lesson in his first spelling book read as follows: "No man can put off the law of God."

When lexicographer Noah Webster published the first American dictionary in 1828, he used Bible verses as definitions. There was no false wall dividing private faith and public service in Webster's day. He was an author, teacher, and preacher who founded a college and served in Congress.

RELIGION AND POLITICS

Lincoln and Webster understood what too many people have forgotten—the importance of faith to the public institutions in a democratic republic. Yet, that connection today is a source of vigorous controversy. A crucial debate rages in the land over the role of religion in public life and the role that religious believers should play in politics.

The religious conservative vote, so vital to the Republican landslide in 1994, is now one of the largest, if not the largest, single voting bloc in the electorate. According to exit polls taken during the 1994 election, fully one-third of all voters were self-identified evangelical and pro-family Roman Catholics. They cast 70% of their ballots for Republicans, compared to 24% for Democrats. The pendulum swing of evangelical voters has transformed the South into a virtually one-party region again, this time favoring the Republicans. The Catholic vote went Republican in 1994 for the first time since Irish Catholics landed on these shores more than a century and a half ago. In 1996, it helped Republicans increase their majorities in the House and Senate, despite Pres. Bill Clinton's resounding reelection.

What Americans are witnessing is nothing less than the largest mobilization of active religious believers in recent memory. If history is any guide, this mobilization is the sign of another period of great transformation in America, for political change in the U.S. always has been rooted in religious upheaval.

Nobel Prize–winning economic historian Robert Fogel argues that the current rightward shift in American politics can be traced to a new American religious revival, a "Fourth Great Awakening." The First Great Awakening, which began in 1730, helped bring on the revolutionary movement; the second in 1800 sparked the antislavery movement; and the third in 1890 gave rise to the progressive impulse. Now, Fogel suggests, the tectonic plates of a religious culture have shifted again, with vast political consequences.

THE POPULARITY OF CONSERVATIVE CHURCHES

Since the mid 1960s, mainline church membership has declined by one-fourth. That, however, is not indicative of a general decline in American faith. It has been more than made up for by the skyrocketing popularity of the conservative and evangelical churches, in which membership has more than doubled. Pentecostal and fundamentalist revivals have converted millions of people. Nesting baby boomers are resuming in droves to the churches and synagogues of their youth. With 15,200,000 members, the Southern Baptist convention has become the largest Protestant denomination in the world.

The result is a complete transformation of America's churchgoing population. Today, the typical American churchgoer is orthodox in faith, traditionalist in outlook, and conservative on cultural and political issues. Yet, as active religious believers move beyond the pews and into public life, a strange and disturbing hostility greets them. Instead of being welcomed into the political arena and into a culture generally acknowledged to be in crisis, they are confronted by an intolerance that frequently curdles into religious bigotry.

This bigotry is manifested in many different settings. In a South Carolina race in 1994, a political candidate said of his opponent, "his only qualifications for office are that he handles snakes and speaks fluently in tongues." In 1995, one candidate for the presidency denounced the nation's religious conservatives as "fringe" and "extremist." In a bizarre twist, a candidate for the U.S. Senate from Massachusetts was denounced in 1995 not because of his stand on issues or ethical problems, but because he once had been an elder in a conservative church. The candidate was Mitt Romney. The accuser was Sen. Edward M. Kennedy.

It was ironic that Kennedy was making his accusations almost 35 years to the day after his brother, then-Sen. John F. Kennedy, was fending off charges that his Roman Catholicism disqualified him from seeking the office of President of the United States. In a speech to the Greater Houston Ministerial Association in 1960, JFK said, "The issue in this campaign should be not what kind of church I believe in, for that should matter only to me. It should be what kind of America I believe in."

DEMONIZING PEOPLE OF FAITH

What kind of America *do* religious conservatives believe in? It is a nation of safe streets, strong families, schools that work, and marriages that stay together, one with a smaller government, lower taxes, and civil rights for all. Most religious conservatives do not countenance discrimination—or special rights—for anyone. Our faith is simple, and our agenda is direct.

For either political party to attack persons holding these views as "fanatics," "extremists," or worse violates a basic American spirit of fairness. More than that, it runs counter to all we are as a nation and all we aspire to be as a people.

For more than 200 years, the U.S. has pursued its vision, maintained a firm foundation, and achieved greatness by honoring God and welcoming people of faith into public life. However, in the years since John F. Kennedy uttered his eloquent warning, we have lost our way. People of faith have become victims of the worst forms of stereotyping, marginalization, and demonology.

Reprinted by permission of Chuck Asay and Creators Syndicate.

As Yale law professor Stephen L. Carter warns, "a culture of disbelief" threatens society. In the place of core beliefs and time-honored values, many of the elites in the academy, media, and government have promoted a different sort of value system—one that presupposes the inability of Americans to care for themselves through a culture of compassion. This system is based not on the relevance and benevolence of God, but on the ability of government to meet every need and provide every solution.

It is not a workable system. Witness the welfare state, once measured by the height of its aspirations and now by the depth of its failures. We read about them every morning in newspapers and see them every evening on television. Social pathologies once imagined only in our darkest nightmares are a daily reality. In 1960, five percent of all children born in the U.S. were born out of wedlock. Today, that figure is 33% and rising. In the largest cities, as many as 67% of the babies are born out of wedlock.

A Carnegie Institute study details the carnage afflicting the nation's young people. One in three adolescents has used illegal drugs before the age of 13. Since 1985, the murder and suicide rates for 10- to 14-year-olds have doubled. Former Secretary of Education Bill Bennett has said that what we do to our kids, they will do to society as adults. That is only partly true; many are not waiting until adulthood before turning to crime and forms of violence that once were unthinkable for children. When a television correspondent asked a group of youngsters what their greatest concern in life was, a seven-year-old African-American raised his hand and said, "Gangs." Imagine that—a seven-year-old boy who goes to bed every night worrying about whether he will be cut down by gangs the next day.

THE ROLE OF FAITH IN PUBLIC LIFE

According to novelist John Updike, "The fact that we live better than our counterparts in Eastern Europe and the former Soviet Union cannot ease the pain that we no longer live nobly." Our culture is testimony to the awful truth of his words. If our inner cities resemble war-torn Bosnia, our children must pass through metal detectors into schools that are armed camps, and one out of every four high school graduates can not read his or her diploma, then we will have failed ourselves, our nation, and God. We can not and must not fail. There is too much at stake.

What is the answer? We must begin by reaffirming the role of faith in public life.

First Amendment rights for religious believers. Let me be clear: I support the separation of church and state. I believe in a nation that is not officially Christian, Jewish, or Muslim. However, I also believe in the right under the First Amendment to freedom of speech, including speech with religious content.

Yet, the same Congress that begins every session with an organized prayer denies that right to students in our public schools. The same Supreme Court that issues rulings from a bench beneath an inscription of the Ten Commandments carved in granite has ruled that those commandments can not be placed on a bulletin board in a public building.

These rulings have real consequences. In 1996, a St. Louis fourth-grader, Raymond Raines, received a week-long detention for bowing his head and praying before lunch. On at least three different occasions, school officials interrupted the student in the middle of his prayer and hauled him off to the principal's office. Finally, the school attempted to extinguish this "politically incorrect" behavior by punishing the boy with detention.

In California, students at a public high school were forbidden from handing out leaflets inviting other pupils to their Bible study group, even though California has a statute specifically allowing students to distribute petitions and literature. In another case, a fifth-grade public school teacher was told by the assistant principal that he could not have a Bible on top of his desk, read the Bible during silent reading period, and have two illustrated books of Bible stories in the classroom library of over 350 volumes. Moreover, in a scene repeated hundreds of times throughout the country every May and June, nervous administrators censor high school students and forbid all references to God and the Bible in graduation speeches.

POLITICAL INVOLVEMENT

Re-entering politics. If we are to reaffirm the role of religion in public life, we must encourage those with strong spiritual values to re-enter politics after too many years of self-imposed retreat. Religious believers must become full citizens, with a place at the table and a voice in the conversation we call democracy. Their involvement should be a source of celebration, not fear. Their participation is not a threat to democracy, but is essential to it. As they enter the political arena, people of faith should not be asked to leave their moral convictions at the door. On issues such as strengthening the family and protecting human life, they are a voice for the voiceless, a defender for the defenseless, and a protector of the innocent.

For Republicans, who have welcomed religious conservatives into their party in recent years, this is a time to decide whether to be the party of Abraham Lincoln and Ronald Reagan or the party of retreat and accommodation; a time to choose between reaffirming moral commitments or succumbing to the timid voices of compromise. I do not speak of a debate over taxes, the budget, or trade, but the most basic and defining issue of all—the sanctity of innocent human life. The Republican Party will not and can not, in my view, remain the majority party it became in 1994 by tearing from the fabric of Republicans' cherished history the heart-felt affirmation of the value of every single human being, including the aged, infirm, and unborn.

BRIDGING DIFFERENCES

I freely acknowledge that not all share this view or the faith that inspires it. That is one of the great privileges of a democracy. I am confident that our views will be tested and our proposals improved by vigorous and open debate. Still, what must be acknowledged is the affirming and healing role faith plays in society.

Just as we acknowledge that at times in the past religion has been twisted to evil ends—such as when the Nazis trumpeted their horrific belief in the superiority of the Aryan race and when Muslim terrorists committed unspeakable acts against innocent civilians while invoking the name of God—we must acknowledge the good ends and enormous blessings of religion. If we can look without prejudice at the real historical record, then together we can bridge the differences that separate us and heal our land.

Recognizing the limits of politics. As important as civic involvement is to a restoration of values, it can not legislate what only can spring from the heart and soul. Politics alone can not restore a land of loving parents, strong marriages, and lullabies sung to sleeping babies and bedtime stories read to wide-eyed children. That work is too important to be left to the government. It is done best by mothers and fathers, churches and synagogues, home and hearth.

It is my hope that, in the days and years to come, this will be an agenda and a vision shared by all Americans. We are a people of many faiths and many races. That is the genius of America. Our motto, E Pluribus Unum, translated means, "Out of many, one." May it be so in our time.

| "Many of liberalism's core values—whether help for the downtrodden or support for peace—derive from the Judeo-Christian tradition."

RELIGIOUS LIBERALISM SHOULD BE PROMOTED

Amy Waldman

In the following viewpoint, Amy Waldman takes issue with the promotion of religious conservatism as a response to America's social and cultural crises. In her opinion, Americans must recognize that the liberal emphasis on social justice for the poor and the disadvantaged evolved out of the Judeo-Christian tradition. Furthermore, Waldman points out, religious liberals have successfully established civil rights laws, antipoverty programs, and foreign policy reforms. She advocates revitalizing a movement of the religious left to strengthen American society and culture. Waldman is an editor of the *Washington Monthly*, a liberal journal of opinion.

As you read, consider the following questions:

1. Why are some liberals uncomfortable with mixing religion and politics, according to Waldman?
2. In the author's opinion, what was radical about Pope John Paul II's message to Americans during his 1995 visit?
3. According to Waldman, why has the religious left recently disappeared from politics?

It was the Christian thing to do. That's what a series of letters to members of Congress from the Reverend Pat Robertson implied. Support Republican tax cuts for wealthy families, the letters said. Support the Republican version of welfare reform, which excluded provisions for child care, health care, and welfare-to-work assistance.

Among the letters' recipients was Representative Glenn Poshard, a fourth-term conservative Democrat from a poor rural district in Illinois. Poshard is a devout Southern Baptist, and he shares some Christian Coalition positions, particularly balancing the budget in seven years and scaling back Medicare. What this former church deacon couldn't figure out, though, was how a tax cut for the wealthy, and the extra cuts in Medicare and programs for the poor it would necessitate, was the Christian thing to do. "I had to ask myself honestly as a Christian, is that appropriate?" says Poshard. "Are [the tax cuts] something that Christ would recommend? I don't think he would." So Poshard went to the House floor to speak. "With all due respect to the Christian Coalition," he asked, "where does it say in the Scriptures that the character of God is to give more to those who have and less to those who have not? . . . If there is one thing evident in the Scriptures, it is that God gives priority to the poor." He quoted Jesus Christ: "When I was thirsty you gave me drink, when I was hungry you fed me . . . When you did it to the least of my brethren, you did it to me."

RELIGIOUS TRADITION AND POLITICS

Poshard's speech was not, in and of itself, notable. For centuries, leaders have drawn on a religious tradition to champion the poor and downtrodden. In America today, however, Poshard's criticism was remarkable. As Republicans claim the halo of Christianity and religious virtue, liberal religious and political leaders have been slow to respond in kind, to show how the Judeo-Christian tradition cannot condone a conservative agenda that rewards the affluent at the expense of the disadvantaged, that takes money from plowshares to forge more swords, and that demands personal responsibility from the poor while excusing the well-off from their social responsibility. Most Americans, raised as Christians or Jews, know and accept the teachings Poshard spoke about. Yet it is the conservative right that has annexed the term "Christianity" in defense of the Republican agenda.

From the religious left there have been only murmurs. "At the moment," says Tom Fox, the editor of the *National Catholic Reporter*, "the religious left is . . . saying 'There's no one else here.

No politicians are with us.'. . . There is virtually no voice in the mainstream today speaking about poverty or the marginalized." Jim Wallis, a Washington, D.C., pastor and author of *The Soul of Politics*, says the progressive religious community couldn't do a Christian Coalition–like voter guide even if it wanted to: "There aren't enough politicians we could support."

Many liberal politicians, meanwhile, complain that religious leaders are not providing the moral support to challenge GOP policies. "I just can't figure it out," says Representative Charles Rangel (D-NY). "I don't see a profile in courage among those who are supposed to speak for Jesus. . . . The cuts that are taking place aren't going to be restored in the next 10 or 20 years. But [liberal religious leaders] now are like deer frozen in the headlights of a car."

THE RELIGIOUS RIGHT

Religious leaders on the right, of course, have been anything but frozen. In the early seventies, a progressive Baptist minister named James Dunn wrote a book on how Christians could become more involved in politics. A few years later, he saw a picture of the Moral Majority's Jerry Falwell reading his book. "We succeeded too well," Dunn, now head of the Joint Baptist Committee on Public Affairs, says, "The wrong people read the book."

Indeed, the succeeding years have seen the demise of the Moral Majority and a stronger phoenix rise from its ashes in the form of the Christian Coalition. In only six years, Robertson and his executive director Ralph Reed have built an organizational machine reminiscent of Mao Tse Tung that aims to build enough clout to swing any election in the nation. With a $24 million annual budget and four million activists, the Coalition is well on its way.

LIBERAL DISCOMFORT WITH RELIGION

As conservatives have successfully used religion to make political inroads, liberals have become increasingly antagonistic to mixing religion and politics. The discomfort with which some liberal intellectuals treat religion stems partly from an understandable concern for the religious provisions of the First Amendment, a concern that some liberals have extended to argue that churches shouldn't speak out on political issues at all. Many liberals also associate religion with intolerance and Elmer Gantry–like evangelism. And some on the left hold the church, particularly the Catholic church, responsible for fueling the pro-life movement. The result, as Stephen Carter points out in his book *Integrity*, is that everyone knows the Pope is firmly against abortion, and a good many liberals resent him for it.

What they don't know, Carter notes, or what they choose to ignore, is his opposition to the death penalty or his repudiation of consumerism or his commitment to helping the poor. Pope John Paul II's message on his 1995 visit seemed downright radical in America's political climate. "Is present-day America becoming less sensitive, less caring toward the poor, the weak, the stranger, and the needy?" he demanded. "It must not!" Similarly, the National Conference of Catholic Bishops recently spoke out harshly against Republican policies—partly because they fear cuts in programs for the poor will encourage abortion, but also, as one Cardinal said, because "the weakest members of society should not bear the greatest burdens" in the effort to balance the budget.

So when secular minds raised on rigid political dichotomies dismiss the Catholic church because of its position on abortion, they throw away the chance to build a coalition on many issues where they have much in common. Abortion is perhaps the religious right's most powerful mobilizing issue; yet the people it attracts aren't the pro–Newt Gingrich caricatures liberals imagine. Stephen Carter notes surveys showing that Christian evangelicals and Roman Catholics are more likely to support liberal economic policies than their supposedly more liberal mainstream or Protestant counterparts and that pro-life advocates are more likely than pro-choice advocates to strongly support government assistance for the unemployed.

That liberals and the Pope have more in common on socioeconomic issues than you might think isn't just coincidence. Many of liberalism's core values—whether help for the downtrodden or support for peace—derive from the Judeo-Christian tradition. Liberals who disdain religion are inadvertently acting like embarrassed adolescents who shun their own parents. For whether or not you believe Jesus was resurrected, he still offers a model for a life of radical social justice. Whether you believe God or men wrote the Bible, it too speaks to how we live. . . .

God on Their Side

The proof of the power is in the history: Dating back at least back to the Quaker abolitionists in the 1830s, American liberals have a much longer—and until the early nineteen-seventies a much stronger—tradition of bringing religion's moral suasion to politics and public policy.

During the Depression, for example, Dorothy Day used the

Catholic church's social teachings, the "preferential option for the poor," to speak out on behalf of the poor, workers, and the unemployed through her *Catholic Worker* newspaper, which inspired a movement of the same name. But it was in the 1960s, with the civil rights movement, that religion's power to transform American society was most obvious. From Catholic bishops who excommunicated segregationists to the rise of civil rights leaders from the black, primarily Baptist churches, the movement was always as much spiritual as it was political.

By rendering faith into action and religious fervor into a passion for social justice, Martin Luther King, Jr. convinced Southern blacks that God (and at least some churches) were on their side, which gave them the strength to protest peaceably. "With this faith," he said in his "I Have a Dream" speech, "we will be able to work together, to pray together, to struggle together, to go to jail together, to stand up for freedom together, knowing that we will be free one day."

A Mistaken Equation on Religion

One of the many historic coalitions that have fallen into disrepair in recent years is the one that united religious and secular progressives. Today, fear of the "religious right" has pushed many secular liberals into opposing virtually any religiously motivated effort to influence public policy debate simply because it is religious. Nothing delights the pooh-bahs of the Christian Coalition more than this mistaken equation. They know they represent only a fraction of the church-, synagogue- and mosque-goers of America. But they desperately want the policy-makers to think they speak for us all. It is this carefully manicured fiction that causes Republic presidential hopefuls to try to outdo one another like vassals flattering the mikado at the court of the Christian Coalition.

Harvey Cox, *Nation*, January 1, 1996.

King also used a biblically based, moral appeal to reach whites; he invoked the inclusive image of "God's children" and explained to white church leaders in his "Letter from Birmingham City Jail" that, "A just law is a man-made code that squares with the moral law or the law of God.". . .

Many of the major liberal economic programs are, in one sense, the use of government as an instrument to fulfill God's will as established in the Old and New Testaments—to lift up the poor, to use an affluent country's resources to help those in need, to shore up the weakest links in the chain that creates a community. That was the spirit of the New Deal; Eleanor Roosevelt once called her husband a "very simple Christian." For Lyndon Johnson, as for John and Robert Kennedy, the War on Poverty and the Great Society weren't just practical exercises in governing; they were about fulfilling the obligations incumbent on religious faith. . . .

In the nineteen-eighties, the religious left had a brief resurgence as Protestant and Catholic churches passionately opposed U.S. aid to the Nicaraguan Contras and the El Salvadoran government. The churches mobilized thousands of members who weren't traditionally liberal or politicized. Opposing communism, they argued, could never justify killing innocent people or funding terrorism. Churches raised millions of dollars and provided sanctuary to refugees, and religious activists testified and protested on Capitol Hill. Many members of Congress attributed their opposition to funding the Contras to the influence of the religious community.

THE FADING OF THE RELIGIOUS LEFT

The campaign for a just Central American policy was important and successful, but it begs a question: Why didn't the churches fire up the same passion about issues confronting Americans at home? Why weren't they sitting in congressional offices protesting conditions in Appalachia and South Central Los Angeles? "[Domestic policy] doesn't hold the glamour of Central America," says Sister Maureen Fieldler of the Quixote Center, a Catholic social action organization in Maryland. "You can't go on a delegation to the inner city." In the same way, the religious left often championed the cause of, say, people with AIDS while ignoring the larger cause of universal health care. The religious left, much like the left at large, sometimes went for radical chic over radical change.

By the time a campaign for universal health care did take hold—during the debate over the Clinton plan in 1993 and 1994—the religious left had long since receded as a major presence on domestic policy issues. After *Roe v. Wade* in 1973, many liberals, led by the feminist movement, turned against the church because of its position on abortion. For the religious right, *Roe v. Wade* sparked political mobilization and fired its ascendency. Later in the decade, Jimmy Carter, a born-again Christian, not only disappointed many liberals but embarrassed them with talk of spiritual "malaise" and of praying for God's guidance when making big decisions. His presidency hastened liberals' flight from religion.

Unfortunately the religious left began to fade just when the economy began to slide; over the years, as the poor got poorer, the religious left proved impotent. While the health-care crisis worsened, for example, religious leaders were first quiet and when they finally acted, ineffective. The religious community lobbied heavily on behalf of universal access to health care; they were precisely the kind of fire-in-their-bellies allies liberals needed. But health-care reform failed dramatically—partly because the other side mobilized greater resources and grassroots opposition (with Christian Coalition help), partly because many religious leaders didn't speak out, and partly because political leaders didn't call on those who did. The coalition splintered over churches' vociferous opposition to any plan that would fund abortion and secular liberals equally adamant attachment to one that would.

THE SILENCE OF RELIGIOUS LIBERALS

Of late, left-leaning religious leaders and devout politicians have spoken too rarely, and too softly, on draconian policies and unsettling economic trends, on violence in the inner city, on the relation between personal responsibility and structural change. Louis Farrakhan motivated hundreds of thousands of black men to march on Washington—what better proof of the need to link spirituality with politics?—but the churches to which those men belong have done little to mobilize protest against GOP policies that could further erode their already weakened communities. "They're basking in a 30-year-old story of Martin Luther King and the black church," says Reverend Eugene Rivers, who heads the Ten Point Coalition in Boston, which aims to inspire local black churches to greater involvement in their communities. Why, in an era when their voices are so crucial, has the religious left become so quiet?

"People should be out in the streets," says Pastor John Steinbruck of Luther Place Church in Washington, D.C. But he's not—for good reason. Upstairs he has three dorms of homeless women and recovering drug addicts. In his basement a group of volunteers supervise activities for the mentally ill. A complex of low-income housing—constructed entirely from money raised by Steinbruck and the church—is being built across the street. "I am consumed with binding up wounds, caring for people," Steinbruck says with frustration. "How much time do I have left [for political activism]? How much energy?"

That's one explanation for the religious left's absence from politics—many of its members are too busy doing social service work to put time into grassroots campaigns. Another is that just as evangelicals during the fifties and sixties saw politics as something dirty, some in mainline religious congregations now fear that political involvement will devolve into a grasp for power, a scramble for money, and thus contradict their most fundamental religious values.

Many religious communities and religious leaders also are unsure whether their role is to provide comfort and celebration for life as it is, or to challenge their followers to change the status quo. That's why liberation theology, a populist interpretation of Scripture that inspired Catholic clergy throughout Latin America and other developing regions to challenge oppressive regimes, was necessary in the first place. Ministers or rabbis who speak out on behalf of the poor risk alienating middle class congregations unless they can provide enough moral fervor to inspire a change of heart. "Most church people are not persuaded or educated as to the social implications of the gospel, because most preachers don't preach it," says Collins Kilburn, the North Carolina director of the National Council of Churches. "I'm 61, and I've been working all my life to make the social gospel more relevant," he says. "I have not been successful."

Other members of mainstream congregations are suspicious that ministers who preach the social gospel are smuggling secular liberal ideology into the church. Those ministers need to show that they are speaking straight from the Old and New Testaments, that liberalism took its cues from those ancient texts and beliefs. . . .

VALUES AND SPIRITUALITY

For liberals, religion offers values as well as spirituality. In a society where we often judge each other on material success—adulating the best ballplayers, the richest entrepreneur, the best-looking model—the Bible provides a wholly different set of criteria: whether you live, as the Jesuits put it, as a "man or woman for others." For believers, the idea that God will judge them, not on who they are but how they act, is a powerful incentive to live differently. Even for nonbelievers, it continuously needles us to strive to be better than we are.

How we treat the least among us—the least important, the least appealing, the least wanted—is the most important test in the Judeo-Christian tradition. On his path to sainthood, God demanded that Saint Francis of Assisi embrace and kiss a leper, whom Francis considered the lowest of all humans. From St. Francis, God exacted compassion harshly: "Half of his putrescent nose had fallen away," Nikos Kazantzakis writes in *God's Pauper*, an imaginative retelling of St. Francis's life. "His hands were without fingers—just stumps; and his lips were an oozing wound. Throwing himself upon the leper, Francis embraced him, then lowered his head and kissed him upon the lips." How many among us would similarly embrace an AIDS patient or a homeless woman who hasn't bathed in weeks? The story of St. Francis moves us, perhaps, just a little closer. . . .

THE NEED FOR A RELIGIOUS LEFT

A religious left is not just vital—it's possible. There are millions of people of faith wanting their better halves appealed to, willing to act, waiting for a vehicle to do so. There are thousands of people acting already. Some small religious lobbying groups—Catholic, Methodist, Lutheran, and more—have been working feverishly to protect federal programs for the disadvantaged. In 1995, for the first time, the theologically Conservative Jewish community lobbied against legislation that would hurt immigrants and the poor, and rabbis were asked to speak out about the disadvantaged during holiday services. "Our tradition has an ethical dimension," says Rabbi Charles Feinberg, who heads the Rabbinical Assembly's Social Action Committee. "They're not just rituals so the Jewish people can survive for the sake of surviving; it's so that we can survive for a higher purpose."

Beyond the Beltway, some black churches are continuing the struggle for social change. In Detroit, for example, at the Baptist Hartford Memorial Baptist Church, throughout his 26-year tenure as pastor, Dr. Charles Adams has exhorted his congregation to scrutinize elected officials and call them to task, to write legislators letters invoking the prophets. The church registers voters, and Dr. Adams makes sure his 8,000 congregants, welfare recipients or college professors, vote: "We preach that you cannot live in this society and not exercise your democratic responsibility."

Then there is Representative Glenn Poshard, exercising not only his democratic but also his religious responsibility. He says many of his colleagues, particularly Southern Democrats, thank him privately for speaking out, but they are scared to do so themselves because the religious right has so much power in their districts. With their silence, that power only grows.

"This is not a question of fighting the Christian Coalition," Poshard says. "It's one Christian taking issue with another on what our faith means. . . . I came out of the same background as the people running the Christian Coalition. . . . When something like a report card goes out so that Christian people—even in my own church—call and say, 'We don't understand why you can't be more Christian in the way you vote,' it hurts me. I have to explain what the budget means, and tell them, 'You think it was un-Christian of me to vote that way. I think it was the most Christian thing to do.'"

"What is needed in a diverse society
is a value system that cultivates
respect and caring for people from
different racial, cultural, and
linguistic backgrounds."

MULTICULTURALISM BENEFITS SOCIETY

Hedy Nai-Lin Chang

Hedy Nai-Lin Chang is codirector of California Tomorrow, a
nonprofit organization committed to building a strong multicultural society. In the following viewpoint, Chang argues that the
people of the United States must develop alliances across racial,
ethnic, and linguistic boundaries. Creating these alliances, she
maintains, requires that people learn to value and respect their
own culture as well as the cultures of other ethnic groups. Fostering an appreciation for cultural differences and discovering
the values that diverse groups share in common will strengthen
and unify America's multiethnic society, Chang contends.

As you read, consider the following questions:
1. What is social capital, according to Chang?
2. In what way is social capital linked to what happens during
   one's childhood, in the author's opinion?
3. For what reasons does Chang support bilingual education?

Adapted, by permission, from Hedy Nai-Lin Chang, "Democracy, Diversity, and Social
Capital," *National Civic Review*, Summer 1997. Copyright ©1997 Jossey-Bass Inc., Publishers.

A mosaic of people from different racial, cultural, and linguistic backgrounds, the United States is one of the most ethnically diverse societies in the world. While this diversity has occurred more rapidly in some states and urban areas, we are, as a country, undergoing a profound demographic transformation. As we move into a century during which there will be no majority ethnic group, our nation is grappling with critical questions about how we function as a society. Will we invest in the well-being of all groups living within our borders and find ways to draw strength from our diversity? Or will we allow our nation to become a society of haves and have-nots, with the demarcations falling primarily along racial lines? Will people of all backgrounds have the opportunity to exercise their rights and responsibilities as members of a democracy? Or will authority and power be consolidated into the hands of a few? Will we become a society torn apart by divisions of race, language, and class, or will we find the common ground that can enable us to remain a cohesive whole?

RESPONDING TO DIVERSITY

How we understand and respond to our diversity is essential to any discussion of social policy in this country, especially how we design strategies to strengthen and foster the existence of social capital. According to Robert Putnam, social capital comprises the features of social life—the network, norms, and trust that enable participants to act together more effectively to pursue shared objectives. Social capital is critical to the well-being of any community because its presence increases people's ability to work together to solve problems that cannot be addressed by individuals working in isolation.

While social capital alone cannot ensure a thriving multiracial democracy, it is essential. In the United States, social capital is needed to ensure cooperation and mutual support among and across people from different racial, cultural, and linguistic groups. Social capital is integral to groups' ability to develop and retain their individual identities and histories, as well as to find the common ground that can bind them together. What we, as a country, must discover is how to nurture social capital in a rapidly changing, increasingly diverse society. This viewpoint will explore this challenge by first examining the origins of social capital and then suggesting possible approaches to sustaining and generating it.

The development of social capital begins with what people learn from their families, neighbors, community institutions, and schools. Some of these concepts are taught directly. Many beliefs and norms are acquired as people hear and observe the words, the actions, the successes, and the challenges encountered by other members of their community.

Social capital is inextricably linked to what happens to people when they are children. How young people are treated has an enormous impact on whether they feel proud of themselves and their community and whether they develop a sense of self-confidence and efficacy. Feeling that you have something to contribute is often a prerequisite for being willing to work with others toward a common goal. Relationships with families and neighbors play a crucial role in shaping whether our youth grow into adults who feel a sense of connection to people from the same and different cultural, linguistic, or racial backgrounds and whether or not they have the skills and language to be able to communicate and interact with others.

Childhood is also a critical time for learning basic values such as respect for elders, commitment to family, and neighborliness. Values lay the foundation for being concerned about more than one's own welfare. Values play a critical role in determining whether networks, norms, and trust advance the health of a community, as opposed to contributing to its decline. A group like the Ku Klux Klan is, for example, a network tied together by strong norms and trusting relationships, but its purposes work against the creation of a strong multiethnic democracy. What is needed in a diverse society is a value system that cultivates respect and caring for people from different racial, cultural, and linguistic backgrounds as well as members of one's own ethnic group or groups.

Social capital is also strengthened when adults have opportunities to reflect upon their values, develop trusting relationships with people who are from the same and different backgrounds, and recognize the assets and strengths they can contribute to their communities. What happens to people as they get older can reinforce their beliefs, or it can force them to question what they learned as children. In some cases, adults find that they must reexamine and even change their beliefs and norms because what they learned earlier is no longer appropriate, given the changes that have occurred in this society.

NURTURING SOCIAL CAPITAL IN A DIVERSE SOCIETY

The challenge for the United States is to design strategies that will foster social capital within and across the diverse groups living within its borders. An underlying assumption of this viewpoint is that both types of social capital are necessary to the well-being of our society as a whole. If a particular group or community has difficulty providing its children and adults with a sense of self-worth and human connection, then society as a whole suffers. At the same time, however, the existence of strong and vibrant subcommunities do not by themselves guarantee a sense of unity across groups.

Described next are several suggestions for nurturing social capital in a diverse society The illustrations of these concepts are based upon my experience working to promote the welfare of children, youth, and families in California, where the demographic changes affecting this nation have been most dramatic. Far from being an exhaustive list, these ideas are intended to stimulate thought and dialogue about what is possible as our country enters the uncharted territory of creating a multicultural democracy.

Reprinted by permission of Kirk Anderson.

First, we should *recognize and support different ways of generating social capital.* While the overall process may be similar, the exact way social capital develops can differ significantly across different groups. In some situations, for example, the entity that plays a major role in affirming values and establishing networks may be a religious institution, whereas, in other places, the workplace or the corner Laundromat may be pivotal. For some groups, mothers or fathers may be primarily responsible for basic socialization and child rearing, while, in others, this role is shared with grandparents or other relatives. Understanding how to nurture social capital in a multiplicity of settings requires being aware of the fact that where, when, and how social capital forms reflects a wide range of factors including economic conditions, racial experience, linguistic background, and cultural practices and beliefs.

Being open to the experiences of people from different ethnic backgrounds is important to understanding how social capital can be sustained. Without this sensitivity and insight, it is all too easy to unwittingly develop public policies that have an adverse impact on the formation of social capital of certain groups. Racial, cultural, and linguistic minorities are in an especially risky position because their norms and practices are often different from the dominant Anglo European norms that generally shape the nature and content of governmental policies and practices.

BILINGUAL EDUCATION

Consider, for example, the increasingly prevalent view that children should be taught English at earlier and earlier ages and that bilingual education should be eliminated. The problem with such a view is that it promotes policies and programs that emphasize only English and may regard the use of children's home language as an obstacle to their development. There is evidence that bilingual education can facilitate the understanding of concepts at an early age and make the child more proficient—even in English—later on. Policies that emphasize English to the exclusion of the home language contribute to and reinforce the likelihood that children will lose their home language. In the United States, English is clearly the language of power and success. It pervades the media, business, and schools. People who speak languages other than English are often ridiculed or treated as having a lower intelligence. The message that English is the most important language is easily and quickly internalized. Children and youth frequently refuse to speak their home languages out of embarrassment or shame, even with their families.

The loss of the home language can have a devastating impact on the development of social capital. Retention of one's home language is often critical to maintaining strong emotional and social ties to family members and other community members as a child, and even into adulthood. First, speaking the home language is essential to family cohesiveness, especially if parents or grandparents do not speak English. Unlike their children, adults are much less likely to have opportunities to learn English, even when they are highly motivated to do so. When children cease to speak their home language, grandparents and parents are in many ways robbed of their capacity to offer guidance, discipline, comfort, and support. Second, language serves as a vehicle for transmitting ideas, beliefs, and customs. Languages often contain words that are impossible to accurately translate. When people cease to speak the language of their family and community, they begin to miss the subtle, but often crucial, nuances of their heritage. Loss of home and community languages significantly reduces the capacity of groups to convey their hopes, values, and traditions to a future generation.

Ironically, many of the people seeking to promote English and eliminate bilingual programs probably perceive themselves as working to increase the levels of social capital across groups by ensuring the existence of a common language. What this example illustrates, however, is that public policies based solely upon the experience of one ethnic group rarely have the intended impact.

IDENTIFYING COMMON VALUES

Second, we should identify common values that can bind us together. This country often seems to be caught between two myths. The first myth is that everyone is alike and therefore requires the same treatment. The problem with this belief is that it leads to policies like the one described earlier, which have an adverse impact because they overlook crucial differences in the ways groups and communities develop. The second myth is that people today are so different that they have nothing in common. This myth perpetuates current fears that society is being torn into separate ethnic enclaves. The challenge before us is to learn to recognize those common values that can bind us together and, at the same time, promote respect and appreciation for our differences.

Establishing some universal values that encompass our differences is necessary for our individual as well as collective success. Such universal values are important because they serve as shared goals that offer groups the opportunity to work together. The process of working together provides people with the opportunity to identify each other's strengths and approaches, as well as to gain a deeper understanding of each other's challenges and issues.

Sometimes the problem is not a lack of common values but a failure to articulate the beliefs we hold in common. One value, for instance, which should and must be reasserted is the right of children to a free and quality public education. This is a fundamental right because education in America is key to success. The right to a public education lies at the heart of the American dream of equal opportunity. It is crucial for individual well-being as well as collective health. A democracy depends on a well-educated populace, yet this right is being challenged today on many fronts. It has been challenged by California's Proposition 187, a successful 1995 ballot initiative that barred undocumented immigrants from receiving publicly funded social services or attending public schools. [A federal judge ruled that Proposition 187 was unconstitutional in November 1997.] In other settings, this right has been threatened by the unthinkably high suspension rates of African American and Latino male students, who are then left with no educational alternative. Another form of attack has been the failure to ensure that all schools, including those operating in low-income communities, have books, materials, and qualified teachers.

FIGHTING AGAINST EACH OTHER

Unfortunately, however, the people and groups struggling to retain their individual or group's right to quality education too often fail to recognize that they in fact share a common goal. Rather than working together to fight for this common right, groups fall into the trap of fighting against each other. In California, a number of African American and legal immigrants living in low-income communities supported Proposition 187 because they felt that allowing undocumented students to go to schools simply takes resources away from their children. But supporting initiatives like Proposition 187 is not what will increase resources to their children. It doesn't, for example, change the fact that schools are suffering from an eroding local tax base of inner cities, or ensure that teachers are equipped to educate an increasingly diverse population. It simply excludes those with the least political power and allows the larger society to avoid facing questions of how to support and develop a viable system of public education. Allowing the right to public education to be eroded for one group may in fact place the children of another group in greater danger. It sets a precedent where we, as a nation, are allowed to discard some children because they are deemed unnecessary for our future.

Rather than waiting to see who will be deemed irrelevant next, people need to join together to reestablish quality education as a basic right rather than a privilege available only to a select few. This right must be upheld by people of all backgrounds, not merely those groups who find the future of their children in danger. Shared values and goals offer this society the chance to reap the benefits of its collective wisdom and foster the potential of all its members.

Third, *we should increase awareness of our interdependency across differences in race, language, and culture.* Promoting social capital requires helping people to understand that their individual welfare is dependent upon the well-being of a larger society. In a diverse society, this means helping people to see themselves as members of a larger, multiethnic community, not just as being tied to those with whom they share a racial, cultural, or linguistic background. For example, one challenge facing the state of California is that more than 50 percent of its children are persons of color, while the voting population is still 80 percent white. Ensuring that resources are available to support the development of strong community institutions, whether they are schools or recreational programs, involves convincing this 80 percent white voting population that their welfare depends upon investing in the well-being of children who may not look like them. . . .

Fourth, *we must invest in leadership development.* Building social capital involves cultivating people who have the skills and capacity to promote and support the implementation of the three strategies discussed earlier. While it is important to recognize and appreciate a wide range of leadership styles and approaches, my experience also suggests that people who are effective in diverse settings tend to share a number of similar qualities including:

- A solid grounding in their individual and group identity, including an understanding of how their background may positively and negatively shape their world view and behavior.
- An understanding of the impact of racial, linguistic, cultural, and class oppression on communities, families, and individuals.
- The ability to assess a situation through multiple lenses and to recognize when another person's perception may be different because of their racial, cultural, socioeconomic, or linguistic experience and history.
- The capacity to appreciate and value different cultures, traditions, and beliefs.
- A commitment to engaging in and modeling power sharing across groups.
- The ability to recognize and affirm common values, goals, and challenges across differences in race, language, and culture.

The responsibility for cultivating these skills and knowledge is a shared one. It is a challenge that must be met by the variety of organizations and people who play a significant role in nurturing the development of young people as well as adults.

147

| "We need to get beyond the point
where race and ethnicity are the
most important factors in the way
we identify ourselves or form
allegiances."

MULTICULTURALISM DOES NOT BENEFIT SOCIETY

Linda Chavez

In the following viewpoint, Linda Chavez argues that multiculturalists incorrectly believe that a person's culture is determined by his or her race or ethnicity. Culture is actually shaped by one's life experiences and not by one's biological ancestry, she maintains. Furthermore, the author contends, highlighting race and ethnicity in public policy disputes only serves to pit various groups against each other, resulting in societal discord. She concludes that Americans must instead recognize that they are of one culture—not a mélange of competing racial and ethnic groups. Chavez is the president of the Center for Equal Opportunity in Washington, D.C., and the author of *Out of the Barrio: Toward a New Politics of Hispanic Assimilation*.

As you read, consider the following questions:

1. According to Chavez, who receives the most prestigious affirmative action slots?
2. In the author's opinion, how does the emphasis on multicultural and bilingual education actually undermine the multiculturalist definition of culture?
3. What kinds of college campus protests reveal the influence of multiculturalism, according to Chavez?

Reprinted, by permission, from Linda Chavez, "Multiculturalism Is Driving Us Apart," *USA Today* magazine, May 1996.

In the name of eliminating discrimination, we continue to pursue policies that define people by color. In schools and universities, at work, at the polling place, even in the courts, race is an important, sometimes deciding, factor in admitting students or devising curricula, hiring or promoting employees, determining political representation, and selecting a jury. It is not only a few white supremacists who promote such policies, but mainstream civil rights advocates as well.

AN OVEREMPHASIS ON ETHNICITY

The crux of the complaint against quotas or other forms of racial or ethnic preferences is that they force both benefactors and beneficiaries to elevate race and ethnicity in importance, which is fundamentally incompatible with reducing racism. It is not possible to argue that race or ethnicity alone entitles individuals to special consideration without also accepting that such characteristics are intrinsically significant.

Those who promote preferential affirmative action programs argue that race and ethnicity are important because they are the basis on which individuals have been, and continue to be, discriminated against. Setting employment or college admission quotas, by this reasoning, simply is a way of compensating for the discrimination that blacks, Hispanics, and some other minority groups face on the basis of their skin color.

However, most programs that confer special benefits to racial and ethnic minorities make no effort at all to determine whether the individuals who will receive them ever have been victims of discrimination. Indeed, the government regulations that govern Federal contractors state explicitly: "Individuals who certify that they are members of named groups (Black Americans, Hispanic Americans, Native Americans, Asian-Pacific Americans, Subcontinental Asian Americans) are to be considered socially and economically disadvantaged."

Such programs are not compensatory, but presumptive; they assume that race equals disadvantage. While there are many blacks, Hispanics, and Asians who have been discriminated against on the basis of their race or ethnicity, there are many others who have not, and still others for whom the discrimination either was trivial or, even if more serious, had no lasting consequences.

PERNICIOUS DISCRIMINATION?

In 1995, at Indiana University following a debate in which I opposed affirmative action, a group of black and Hispanic students approached me to complain that I was not sensitive enough to the discrimination they said they faced daily on campus. I asked them to give me some examples. Only two spoke. The first, a young black woman, told me her father was a surgeon who makes more than $300,000 a year, but that her economic status doesn't protect her from the prejudice of her teachers. When I asked her to describe how that prejudice manifested itself, she said none of her professors would give above a "B" to any minority student. I pushed her a little further, asking whether that meant that a student who scored 98% on an exam would be given a "B" rather than a deserved "A." At that point, she dropped the issue with a dismissive, "You just don't understand."

A second student, a Mexican-American woman, said that she has to deal with discrimination every day. She cited as an example that her Spanish teacher expects her to do better than the other students because she is presumed to know Spanish. I was sympathetic with her frustration, since I am aware that most third-generation Hispanics speak only English—like third-generation Italians, Jews, Germans, and other ethnic groups in the U.S. Nevertheless, although being presumed to speak your ancestral language may be annoying, it hardly constitutes pernicious discrimination.

In fact, what ethnic or religious minority has not suffered its share of slights and prejudices? Certainly, Jews and Asians have faced significant levels of bigotry at certain points in their history in the U.S. Jews often were the victims of private discriminatory actions, and Asians historically were the target of both private and state-sponsored exclusion and bias. The Chinese, for instance, were not allowed to become citizens, own property, or enter certain professions, or even to immigrate at all for certain periods of time. During World War II, Japanese-Americans had their property confiscated and were removed forcibly from their homes and interned in camps in the West. Nonetheless, despite persistent discrimination, these groups, on average, have excelled in this society, and it is difficult to argue that they are entitled to compensatory, preferential affirmative action on the basis of any current disadvantage.

It is true that blacks and, to a lesser degree, Hispanics are far more likely to face present disadvantage, some of it (though a declining share) the result of past discrimination. Again, though, many affirmative action programs make little effort to distinguish among potential beneficiaries on the basis of actual disadvantage, preferring instead to rely on race or ethnicity *per se* in awarding benefits.

Some of the most prestigious affirmative action slots—such as those at Ivy League universities, Fortune 500 corporations, or Wall Street law firms—go to middle- and upper-class blacks and Hispanics, who suffer no clear disadvantage compared with their white counterparts. For instance, a recent study at the University of California, Berkeley, found that, on average, black, Hispanic, and Asian students admitted through affirmative action guidelines come from families whose median income actually is higher than the national average. Affirmative action recipients frequently are the graduates of elite prep schools, universities, and professional schools. Increasingly, advocates of this select type of affirmative action eschew traditional arguments about discrimination or disadvantage, opting to emphasize the presumed benefits of racial and ethnic diversity.

CULTURE AS WEAPON

What does this diversity imply? The current scientific consensus suggests that race or ethnicity is nothing more than a description of broad morphology of skin, hair, and eye color; bone structure; and hair type—hardly the basis for making moral claims or distinctions. If race and ethnicity, stripped of their power to demand retribution, represent nothing more than a common ancestry and similar physical attributes, culture, on the other hand, evinces something more controversial and enduring. Not surprisingly, practitioners of the politics of race have seized on culture as their new weapon. Americans—of all races—have grown tired of affirmative action. Many of those who still support racial preferences, such as Yale law professor Stephen Carter, admit that those preferences have been a mixed blessing for the beneficiaries, conferring tangible benefits, but often undermining self-confidence. The politics of race requires a new rationale and a new vocabulary. Multiculturalism supplies both.

Race-conscious policies now permeate not only employment and education, but also the courts and even the democratic process itself. Race or ethnicity often determines political representation and establishes voting procedures. In addition, the list of groups eligible to benefit continues to grow and now embraces even the most recent immigrants to America, who, by definition, have suffered no past discrimination. As the policies and the beneficiaries expand, so has their rationale.

The compensatory model has given way to one based on culture, which alleviates the necessity of proving past discrimination or present disadvantage. The demand to redress past or present wrongs evolves into the imperative to enhance and preserve culture. America becomes not simply a multi-racial, multi-ethnic society made up of individuals of different backgrounds—some of whom have suffered discrimination because of their color—but a *multicultural* nation. The distinction is an important one. It implies that Americans differ not only in skin color and origin, but in values, mores, customs, temperament, language—all those attributes that endow culture with meaning. Indeed, multiculturalism questions the very concept of an *American* people. It replaces affirmative action as the linchpin in the politics of race with a much more profound power to shape how all Americans, not just racial and ethnic minorities, think of themselves and conceive the nation.

THE DANGERS OF MULTICULTURALISM

It is not simply that radical multiculturalism is bad education, trendy education, education lacking any real substance. All these things it is; but as bad as this is, today's multiculturalism—this new and deluded education in separatism—threatens America with consequences even more far-reaching and pernicious than the "dumbing down" of its children. Because, while radical multiculturalism might not teach today's students even the simplest facts about American history, what it does teach them threatens to bring on them only more separatism, hostility, and violence, leading in time, perhaps, to a new civil war.

Thomas K. Lindsay, *Journal of Social, Political, and Economic Studies*, Fall 1995.

Multiculturalists insist on treating race or ethnicity as if they were synonymous with culture. They presume that skin color or national origin, which are immutable traits, determine values, mores, language, and other cultural attributes, which, of course, are learned. In the multiculturalists' world view, African-Americans, Puerto Ricans, or Chinese-Americans living in New York City, for instance, share more in common with persons of their ancestral group living in Lagos, San Juan, or Hong Kong than they do with other New Yorkers who are white. Culture becomes a fixed entity, transmitted, as it were, in the genes, rather than through experience.

Such convictions lead multiculturalists to conclude that, in the words of Molefi Kete Asante, a guru of the multicultural movement, "There is no common American culture." The logic is simple, if wrongheaded. Since Americans (or, more often, their forebears) hail from many different places, each with its own specific culture, the U.S. must be multicultural. Moreover, they claim, it is becoming more so every day as new immigrants bring their cultures with them when they come to the U.S.

MULTICULTURALISM AND EDUCATION

Indeed, multiculturalists hope to ride the immigrant wave to greater power and influence. They certainly have done so in education. The influx of non-English-speaking children into public schools has given added impetus to the multicultural movement. Approximately 2,300,000 youngsters who can not speak English well now attend public school, an increase of 1,000,000 since 1989. The Los Angeles Unified School District alone offers instruction to 160,000 students in Spanish, Armenian, Korean, Cantonese, Tagalog, Russian, and Japanese. In New York, students come from 167 different countries, speaking 120 separate languages. The costs for such programs are astronomical—more than $300,000,000 a year for 126,000 pupils in New York. Multicultural advocates cite the presence of such children to demand bilingual education and other multicultural services. Federal and state governments literally spend billions of dollars on these initiatives, although an exact estimate of total outlay is difficult to obtain since it is allocated across several programs and layers of government.

The multiculturalists' emphasis on education, though, undercuts their own argument that culture is inextricable from race or national origin. The multiculturalists are acutely aware of just how fragile cultural identification is. If they were not, they would be less adamant about preserving and reinforcing it. The current emphasis on Afrocentric curricula for black elementary and secondary students, for instance, would be unnecessary if race itself conferred culture. Nor would multiculturalists insist on teaching immigrant children in their native language, instructing them in the history and customs of their native land, and imbuing them with reverence for their ancestral heroes, if ethnicity and national origin alone were antidotes to the appeal of American culture.

RESISTING ASSIMILATION

Multiculturalists haven't lost faith in the power of assimilation. If anything, they seem to believe that, without a heavy dose of multicultural indoctrination, immigrants won't be able to resist assimilation. They are right, though it remains to be seen whether anything, including the multiculturalists' crude methods, ultimately will detour immigrants from the assimilation path.

The urge to assimilate traditionally has been overpowering in the U.S., especially among the children of immigrants. Only groups that maintain strict rules against intermarriage and other social contact with persons outside the group, such as Orthodox Jews and the Amish, ever have succeeded in preserving distinct, full-blown cultures within American society after one or two generations have been living here. It is interesting to note that religion seems to be a more effective deterrent to full assimilation than the secular elements of culture, including language.

Although many Americans worry that Hispanic immigrants, for example, are not learning English and therefore will fail to assimilate into the American mainstream, there is little evidence that this is the case. As already noted, a majority of Hispanics speak only English by the third generation in the U.S., and are closer to other Americans on most measures of social and economic status than they are to Hispanic immigrants. On one of the most rigorous gauges of assimilation—intermarriage—Hispanics rank high. About one-third of young, third-generation Hispanics marry non-Hispanic whites, a pattern similar to that of young Asians. Even for blacks, exogamy rates, which have been quite low historically, are going up. About three percent of blacks now marry outside their group, though the rate in the western states is much higher—17% among black males marrying for the first time.

MULTICULTURALISM ON CAMPUS

The impetus for multiculturalism is not coming from immigrants—even among groups such as Hispanics and Asians—but from their more affluent and (ironically) assimilated native-born counterparts in their ethnic communities. The proponents most often are the elite, best-educated, and most successful members of their respective racial and ethnic groups. Not surprisingly, college campuses are fertile recruiting grounds, where the most radical displays of multiculturalism take place.

In May, 1993, for instance, a group of Mexican-American students at UCLA, frustrated that the university would not elevate the school's 23-year-old Chicano studies program to full department status, stormed the campus faculty center, breaking windows and furniture and causing $500,000 in damage. During the same month, a group of Asian-American students at the University of California, Irvine, went on a hunger strike to pressure administrators into hiring more professors to teach Asian-American studies courses there. These were not immigrants or even, by and large, disadvantaged students, but middle-class beneficiaries of their parents' or grandparents' successful assimilation into the American mainstream.

The protesters' actions had almost nothing to do with any effort to maintain their ethnic identity. For the most part, such students probably never thought of themselves as anything but American before they entered college. According to the Berkeley study cited earlier, most Hispanic and Asian students "discovered" their ethnic identity after they arrived on campus. Speaking of Asian students, the researchers reported: "After being around [the University of California] for one or two years, students who were integrated into predominantly white worlds of friendship and association in high school report a shift towards having predominantly Asian American friends, roommates, or affiliations with an Asian American organization."

The same was true for other groups as well, including blacks. "On arrival on the Berkeley campus, these students are surprised to discover themselves no longer the 'token black person.'. . . These students experience a new kind of pressure: it comes from other African American students on campus, and it is experienced as pressure to make decisions about friends, networks, even who you sit with at lunch, on the basis of race."

Many of these students learn to define themselves as victims as well. As one Mexican-American freshman summed it up, she was "unaware of the things that have been going on with our people, all the injustices we've suffered, how the world really is. I thought racism didn't exist here, you know, it just comes to light." The researchers went on to note that all "students of color" had difficulty pinpointing exactly what constituted this "subtle form of the new racism." Instead of empirical evidence, "There was much talk of certain facial expressions, or the way people look, and how white students 'take over the class' and speak past you."

If terms like racism and discrimination can be applied to such innocuous behavior, what words can be used to describe the real thing? As author George Orwell said in his 1946 essay, "Politics and the English Language," "if thought corrupts language, language can also corrupt thought." Misusing words like racism undermines the very legitimacy of the concept.

A STEP BACKWARD

The re-racialization of American society that is taking place in the name of multiculturalism is not a progressive movement, but a step backward to the America that existed before Brown v. Board of Education and the passage of the major civil rights laws of the 1960s. We are at a critical juncture in our history. Even if we are not, as the multiculturalists claim, about to become a majority minority nation, racial and ethnic diversity in our population is increasing. If we allow race and ethnicity to determine public policy, we invite the kind of cleavages that will pit one group against another in ways that can not be good for the groups themselves or the society we all must live in.

The more diverse we become, the more crucial it is that we commit ourselves to a shared, civic culture. The distinguishing characteristic of American culture always has been its ability to incorporate so many disparate elements into a new whole. While conservative philosopher Russell Kirk was indisputably right that the U.S. owes much of its culture to Great Britain— our legal tradition, particularly the concept of the rule of law, our belief in representative government, and certainly our language and literature—American assimilation always has entailed some give and take. American culture itself has been enriched by what individual groups brought to it.

Yet, it is more important that all of us—no matter where we come from or what circumstances brought us or our ancestors here—think of ourselves as Americans if we are to retain the sense that we are one people, not simply a conglomeration of different and competing groups. It is nonsense to think we can do so without being clear about our purposes.

We can by acknowledging that it is more important for immigrant children to learn English than to maintain their native language, although the two not necessarily are mutually exclusive. We should make sure that American students have a firm grasp of the history of this nation, the people who helped build it, and the institutions and principles on which the U.S. was founded. We should be careful not to repeat past errors, when American history courses conveniently excluded facts, but neither should history become simply an exercise in building the self-esteem of those who previously were left out. Finally, we need to get beyond the point where race and ethnicity are the most important factors in the way we identify ourselves or form allegiances. The principles and values that unite us remain far more important than our differences in ancestry, a lesson that bears repeating in our schools and universities.

PERIODICAL BIBLIOGRAPHY

The following articles have been selected to supplement the diverse views presented in this chapter. Addresses are provided for periodicals not indexed in the *Readers' Guide to Periodical Literature*, the *Alternative Press Index*, the *Social Sciences Index*, or the *Index to Legal Periodicals and Books*.

David Aikman
"Pilgrims' Progress," *Policy Review*, July/August 1997.

Edgar F. Beckham
"Diversity Opens Doors to All," *New York Times*, January 5, 1997.

Harvey Cox
"The Transcendent Dimension," *Nation*, January 1, 1996.

Thomas J. Famularo
"The Intellectual Bankruptcy of Multiculturalism," *USA Today*, May 1996.

Isaac Kramnick and R. Laurence Moore
"Is God a Republican?" *American Prospect*, September/October 1996.

Gloria J. Leitner
"A Legacy from Parent to Child," *Humanist*, March/April 1997.

John Leo
"A No-Fault Holocaust," *U.S. News & World Report*, July 21, 1997.

Patrick McCormick
"Religious Right and Wrong in America," *U.S. Catholic*, April 1996.

Jack Miles
"Religion Makes a Comeback. (Belief to Follow.)," *New York Times Magazine*, December 7, 1997.

Richard J. Mouw
"Tolerance Without Compromise," *Christianity Today*, July 15, 1996.

Anne Phillips
"Why Worry About Multiculturalism?" *Dissent*, Winter 1997.

Paul Ray
"The Great Divide: Prospects for an Integral Culture," *YES! A Journal of Positive Futures*, Fall 1996. Available from PO Box 10818, Bainbridge Island, WA 98110.

Robert L. Simonds
"Common Ground with the Religious Right," *Education Digest*, January 1997.

Mark Tooley
"Religious Left Coalitions," *Crisis*, July/August 1996. Available from PO Box 10559, Riverton, NJ 08076-0559.

John Tusa
"They Say God Is Dead. Why Won't He Lie Down?" *Index on Censorship*, July/August 1996.

CHAPTER 4

SHOULD GOVERNMENT REGULATE CULTURAL VALUES?

Chapter Preface

The National Endowment for the Arts (NEA), a government agency that uses tax revenues to fund artists and nonprofit arts organizations, has been the subject of much controversy in the 1980s and 1990s. Critics have charged that the NEA should be eliminated because it often subsidizes offensive, pornographic art and art with a left-wing cultural bias. NEA supporters maintain that the agency provides needed funds to orchestras, dance companies, and community arts agencies; furthermore, they contend, government arts subsidies should not be contingent on the content of art.

In 1990, Congress passed a law requiring the NEA to consider "general standards of decency and respect for the diverse beliefs and values of the American public." This legislation was challenged in a lawsuit by a group of four performance artists who claimed that such "decency" rules violated freedom of expression. They argued that the law allowed the NEA to deny funding simply "because of the artist's political or social message." Sidney Yates, the founder of the NEA, agreed, commenting that "there is such a thing as controversial art that is not pornographic. Artists have always been willing to walk new roads away from existing patterns and I think that's essential. . . . What [NEA critics] are talking about is controlling the content of art and I don't think government should do that."

In June 1998, however, the Supreme Court ruled in favor of the 1990 law. Justice Sandra Day O'Connor contends that, in the Court's official opinion, the 1990 legislation is not a violation of First Amendment rights. This law does not allow the government to censor art, she maintains, it simply permits the government to use discretion in its funding decisions. Supporters of the Supreme Court ruling assert, moreover, that citizens do not deserve to have their tax money spent on art that offends their sensibilities. Artists who are denied NEA funding have access to multiple sources of private funding, many commentators point out.

Political and social analysts continue to dispute the government's role in contentious cultural issues such as arts funding, abortion, and bilingual education. The following chapter includes commentaries on these topics from authors representing various points on the political spectrum.

"Ultimately, no matter how difficult
a moral decision any individual
abortion might be, that decision
rightly belongs to a woman and her
doctor."

GOVERNMENT SHOULD PROTECT WOMEN'S RIGHT TO ABORTION

The Progressive

One of the primary controversies in America's culture wars is abortion. The following viewpoint by the editors of the *Progressive* is a response to the twenty-fifth anniversary of *Roe v. Wade*, the 1973 Supreme Court decision that legalized abortion. The editors argue that although abortion remains legal, recent legislation has increasingly restricted access to the procedure, revealing the government's devaluing of women's right to reproductive choice. These restrictions, they maintain, include limited or banned access to abortion for military servicewomen and prisoners, parental consent laws, and mandatory waiting periods. Pro-choice activists must avoid complacency if they wish to encourage the government to secure continued access to safe and legal abortions, the *Progressive* editors conclude. The *Progressive* is a monthly journal of left-wing political opinion.

As you read, consider the following questions:
1. What percentage of U.S. counties have no abortion provider, according to the authors?
2. According to the *Progressive* editors, what percentage of U.S. medical schools regularly provide abortion training?
3. When did the first bans on abortions occur, according to the authors?

Reprinted from "Roe v. Wade at Twenty-five," editorial, The Progressive, February 1998, by permission of The Progressive, 409 E. Main St., Madison, WI 53703.

The pro-choice movement is celebrating the twenty-fifth anniversary of *Roe v. Wade*, the landmark Supreme Court decision making abortion legal.

But it's not the happiest party. Women are having more and more difficulty getting access to safe abortions. "In the twenty-five years since the *Roe v. Wade* decision, almost all the steps have been backward," says Gloria Feldt, president of the Planned Parenthood Federation of America. "The Supreme Court has repeatedly reaffirmed the basic right to abortion, but it has also given legislative bodies increasing authority to restrict access."

"The choice to have an abortion is more difficult for women today than at any time since *Roe v. Wade*," agrees Kate Michelman, president of the National Abortion and Reproductive Rights Action League (NARAL). "1997 was a dramatic year. It was probably the worst."

LIMITED ACCESS TO ABORTION

In 1997, the 105th Congress banned access to privately funded abortions at overseas military hospitals for servicewomen and military dependents, banned abortions for women in federal prison, prohibited insurance for federal employees from covering abortions, and prohibited abortions for Medicaid recipients except in cases of life endangerment, rape, or incest.

The new law affecting women in the military prohibits servicewomen from getting abortions in military hospitals, even if they pay for them. This is particularly onerous for female soldiers stationed in countries where abortion is illegal.

Feldt says some prisons go so far as to refuse to transport the prisoner even if Planned Parenthood agrees to do the abortion free of charge.

The infringement of the right to abortion comes not just from government, but from the private sector as well. Catholic hospitals—and even some secular ones—are gobbling up other hospitals and closing off the abortion option.

TILTING THE DEBATE

The campaign against third-trimester "partial-birth abortion" has also tilted the debate. These late-term abortions are relatively rare and often occur when something has gone terribly wrong with the pregnancy or when the mother's health is in danger.

Legislation inspired by the partial-birth-abortion debate would pave the way for overturning *Roe*. "While they have told you that those bans protect against a gruesome procedure that occurs in the third trimester of a pregnancy, the definition these laws use reaches any safe and common method of abortion from the end of the first trimester onward," says Catherine Weiss, the director of the American Civil Liberties Union's Reproductive Freedom Project. "While it has been sold as a ban on a rare, late procedure, none of the bans have limits in terms of when the ban applies. They do not describe a discrete procedure. They describe abortion."

Most of the damage to *Roe v. Wade* is happening at the state level. In 1997, state legislatures introduced 405 anti-choice measures (compared with 220 in 1996). States enacted fifty-five (compared with fourteen in 1996).

According to Planned Parenthood, 84 percent of all U.S. counties now have no abortion provider, and many states are imposing such restrictions as parental consent and mandatory waiting periods.

Waiting periods are especially troublesome to poor women and those who live in rural areas. Many have to travel to other states and take days off from work to get to an abortion provider.

"If you have to appear at an abortion clinic twice and you have to travel 500 miles, you've got big problems," says Weiss. She cites stories of women who take Greyhound buses into the city to get abortion counseling, then return to the station to sleep at night in order to save money on motel costs until they can have the abortion.

Choosing to have an abortion is a very difficult decision for a woman to make. Many of these new restrictions are designed to make it even more wrenching. Ultimately, no matter how difficult a moral decision any individual abortion might be, that decision rightly belongs to a woman and her doctor.

A DIFFERENT POLITICAL CLIMATE

Elizabeth Karlin, medical director of the Women's Medical Center in Madison, Wisconsin, says the atmosphere outside her clinic has changed. Several years ago, crowds of protesters greeted her every day. Now, she says, "they don't need to have demonstrations outside my offices because they have the governor, they have the Department of Health and Human Services, they have the state on their side." Wisconsin now requires two in-person visits, counseling, and a twenty-four-hour waiting period for all women who have abortions. The most recent state budget also would exclude the use of public funds "for direct referral, or [referral] through an intermediary" for abortion services. Bills pending in the Wisconsin legislature include one that would create twenty new crimes against a fetus and make it a criminal offense to destroy a fertilized egg, another that would allow officials to detain a pregnant woman to protect the fetus, and another that would permit pharmacists to refuse to fill any prescription they oppose for moral or religious reasons.

Reprinted by permission of Ann Telnaes.

Medical schools are a battleground as well, since fewer and fewer of them teach abortion procedures. According to a recent study by the Alan Guttmacher Institute, about one out of ten obstetric and gynecology programs in the country currently requires abortion training, and only 12 percent of medical schools make a regular practice of teaching it. Approximately one-third offer no training at all. The average age of doctors practicing abortion is rising. "Those doctors remember what it was like when abortion was illegal and women were dying," says Gloria Feldt of Planned Parenthood. Today, many young doctors would rather not take up a practice that requires wearing a bulletproof vest to work.

"It is possible that *Roe* could be overturned in the courts or overturned legislatively in our lifetime," says Feldt. "That's not inevitable. It will happen only if we let it happen. At this time, it's the anti-choice crowd that is loud and organized. The pro-choice crowd is complacent. A lot of the young ones don't understand what it was like."

THE HISTORY OF ABORTION

When Abortion Was Illegal, a documentary produced and directed by Dorothy Fadiman, is an antidote to amnesia. The film documents the history of abortion in the United States before *Roe v. Wade*. Early in the Republic, abortion was generally legal, Fadiman reports. Until the mid-1800s, the state and the church allowed abortions "if they occurred before 'quickening,' when the mother first perceived fetal movement."

Strict prohibitions on abortion started to come about when doctors began to professionalize, and to root out their competition—midwives. At about the same time, society began to condemn women who sought abortions as selfishly shirking their duty.

"By the turn of the [twentieth] century," Fadiman concludes, "both abortion and birth control were illegal in most states."

Against the law or not, thousands and thousands of American women still had abortions each year for the next century. The women who pursued illegal abortions, or induced abortions themselves, suffered all kinds of horrible complications, and many of them died.

One woman in the film, identified only as Rosalie, tells the story of an abortion she experienced as a teenager, when the procedure was still illegal. "The day came and they took me to a motel several miles from Boise. It was a dirty motel and I was alone with this woman. I remember what she looked like really well. She was dirty, too. And not friendly . . . really divorced from the proceedings. She gave me a cervical puncture. I remember the steel tool. Then she told me to go and that there would be blood, but I would be all right. But the fact is that I didn't abort. I just bled a lot. It was incredibly painful and I got a bad infection. They [the people responsible for the botched abortion] started to look for a doctor because I kept bleeding and bleeding and not aborting. The doctor, he gave me some medication to make me abort. I aborted at home, so that if he were caught, he would be able to prove that the process had been initiated before he became involved."

Despite the recent setbacks to reproductive choice, we haven't yet returned to the dark days before abortion was legal. But unless the pro-choice movement fights for continued access to safe, legal abortion, it won't matter whether *Roe v. Wade* stands or falls.

"There can be little doubt that, left to the normal workings of democracy, abortion laws would generally be protective of infants in the womb."

GOVERNMENT SHOULD PROTECT THE RIGHT TO LIFE

National Review

Abortion continues to be a central issue in America's culture wars. In the following viewpoint, written in response to the twenty-fifth anniversary of the 1973 Supreme Court decision legalizing abortion, the editors of National Review contend that abortion is a form of licensed killing that has damaged the family, the legal system, and the practice of medicine. The pro-abortion movement has achieved its ends by deceiving the public about the causes and effects of legalized abortion, the authors argue. Moreover, they maintain, the sanctioning of abortion has led society to consider allowing previously inconceivable practices such as euthanasia and experimentation on embryos. The authors conclude that the moral values of the pro-life movement, which stand in sharp contrast to the spirit of abortion laws, deserve governmental and judicial support. National Review is a biweekly journal of conservative opinion.

As you read, consider the following questions:

1. According to National Review, abortion has resulted in how many deaths?
2. How could the argument for abortion be used to support infanticide, in the authors' opinion?
3. According to National Review, how has abortion corrupted liberalism?

A quarter-century has passed since the Supreme Court struck down the laws of every state in the nation, in the name of a constitutional right to abortion it had just discovered. In *Roe v. Wade*, the Court prohibited any regulation of abortion in the first trimester, allowed only regulations pertaining to the health of the mother in the second, and mandated that any regulation in the third make an exception for maternal health. In the companion case of *Doe v. Bolton*, the Court insisted on the broadest definition of health—economic, familial, emotional. Legal scholar Mary Ann Glendon describes the result as the most radical pro-abortion policy in the democratic world. It permits abortion at any stage of pregnancy, for any reason or for no reason. It has licensed the killing of some 35 million members of the human family so far.

A MOVEMENT BORN IN LIES

The abortion regime was born in lies. In Britain (and in California, pre-*Roe*), the abortion lobby deceptively promoted legal revisions to allow "therapeutic" abortions—and then defined every abortion as "therapeutic." The abortion lobby lied about Jane Roe, claiming her pregnancy resulted from a gang rape. It lied about the number of back-alley abortions. Justice Harry A. Blackmun relied on fictitious history to argue, in *Roe*, that abortion had never been a common-law crime.

The abortion regime is also sustained by lies. Its supporters constantly lie about the radicalism of *Roe*: even now, most Americans who "agree with *Roe v. Wade*" in polls think that it left third-term abortions illegal and restricted second-term abortions. They have lied about the frequency and "medical necessity" of partial-birth abortion. Then there are the euphemisms: "terminating a pregnancy," abortion "providers," "products of conception." "The fetus is only a potential human being"—as if it might as easily become an elk. "It should be between a woman and her doctor"—the latter an abortionist who has never met the woman before and who has a financial interest in her decision. This movement cannot speak the truth.

Roe's supporters said at the time that the widespread availability of abortion would lead to fewer unwanted pregnancies, hence less child abuse; it has not. They said that fewer women would die from back-alley abortions; the post-1940s decline in the number of women who died from abortions, the result of antibiotics, actually slowed after *Roe*—probably because the total number of abortions rose. They said it would reduce illegitimacy and child poverty, predictions that now seem like grim jokes.

DEVALUING HUMAN LIFE

Pro-lifers were, alas, more prescient. They claimed the West had started down the slippery slope of a progressive devaluation of human life. After the unborn would come the elderly and the infirm—more burdens to others; more obstacles to others' goals; probably better off dead, like "unwanted children." And so now we are debating whether to allow euthanasia, whether to create embryos for experimental purposes, whether to permit the killing of infants about to leave the womb.

And what greater claim on our protection, after all, does that infant have a moment after birth? He still lacks the attributes of "personhood"—rationality, autonomy, rich interactions—that pro-abortion philosophers consider the preconditions of a right to life. The argument boils down to this assertion: If we want to eliminate you and you cannot stop us, we are justified in doing it. Might makes right. Among intellectuals, infanticide is in the first phase of a movement from the unthinkable to the arguable to the debatable to the acceptable.

| BANNING ABORTION WOULD BE LEGITIMATE

Efforts to ban abortion have often been compared to Prohibition, with the conclusion that just as the latter could not be enforced, neither could the former. But the analogy is a weak one. Prohibition, for one thing, involved the effort to ban something (alcohol) which is good in itself even though abused by some, whereas pro-lifers are trying to ban something which is intrinsically evil, under any and all circumstances. Furthermore, there *was* in fact a national consensus in support of Prohibition—without such a consensus a constitutional amendment could never have been passed. Despite that, it could not be enforced. I would speculate that its unenforceability had a great deal to do with its inherent inconsistency with human nature and hence with the common good. It was a violation of the common good sanctioned by a democratic majority, a consensus, which did not give it any legitimacy. A ban on abortion, even opposed by a democratic majority, would be legitimate because it would represent the effort to restore the common good.

George A. Kendall, *Wanderer*, April 25, 1996.

Everything abortion touches, it corrupts. It has corrupted family life. In the war between the sexes, abortion tilts the playing field toward predatory males, giving them another excuse for abandoning their offspring: She chose to carry the child; let her pay for her choice. Our law now says, in effect, that fatherhood has no meaning, and we are shocked that some men have learned that lesson too well. It has corrupted the Supreme Court, which has protected the abortion license even while tacitly admitting its lack of constitutional grounding. If the courts can invent such a right, unmoored in the text, tradition, or logic of the Constitution, then they can do almost anything; and so they have done. The law on everything from free speech to biotechnology has been distorted to accommodate abortionism. And abortion has deeply corrupted the practice of medicine, transforming healers into killers.

Most of all, perhaps, it has corrupted liberalism. For all its flaws, liberalism could until the early Seventies claim a proud history of standing up for the powerless and downtrodden, of expanding the definition of the community for whom we pledge protection, of resisting the idea that might makes right. The Democratic Party has casually abandoned that legacy. Liberals' commitment to civil rights, it turns out, ends when the constituency in question can offer neither votes nor revenues.

THE PRO-LIFE MOVEMENT

Abortion-on-demand has, however, also called into being in America a pro-life movement comprising millions of ordinary citizens. Their largely unsung efforts to help pregnant women in distress have prevented countless abortions. And their political witness has helped maintain a pro-life ethic that has stopped millions more. The conversions of conscience have almost all been to the pro-life side—Bernard Nathanson, Nat Hentoff, Elizabeth Fox-Genovese. The conversions of convenience have mostly gone the other way, mainly politicians who wanted to get ahead in the Democratic Party—Jesse Jackson, Dick Gephardt. The fight against abortion has resulted in unprecedented dialogue and cooperation between Catholics and Protestants, first on moral values and now increasingly on theological ones. It has helped transform the Republican Party from a preserve of elite WASPs into a populist and conservative party.

True, few politicians of either party—with honorable exceptions like Henry Hyde, Chris Smith, Jesse Helms, Bob Casey, Charles Canady, and Rick Santorum—have provided leadership in the struggle. Not because opposition to abortion is unpopular—throughout the *Roe* era, 70 per cent of the public has supported laws that would prohibit 90 per cent of abortions—but because politicians, and even more the consultants and journalists and big-money donors to whom they listen, tend to move in elite circles where accepting abortion is *de rigueur* and pro-life advocacy at best an offense against good taste. Since everyone they know favors legal abortion, they understandably conclude that everyone does. But there is progress even here. The pro-abortion intellectual front is crumbling. Supporters of the license increasingly concede that what they support is, indeed, the taking of human life. Pro-lifers, their convictions rooted in firmer soil, have not had to make reciprocal concessions.

There can be little doubt that, left to the normal workings of democracy, abortion laws would generally be protective of infants in the womb. The main obstacle on our path to a society where every child is welcomed in life and protected in law, then, remains what it has always been: the Supreme Court. There abortionism is well entrenched; and in 1997 the Court appeared to slam the door on the legal possibility of a congressional override of its decisions on abortion or anything else. By defining a practice at odds with our deep and settled moral convictions as part of the fundamental law of the land, the Supreme Court has created a slow-motion constitutional crisis. This is what comes of courting death.

| "*[Hispanic parents]* think learning to read, write and speak English is the single most important goal of education."

GOVERNMENT SHOULD PROMOTE INSTRUCTION IN ENGLISH

Linda Chavez

Many people support bilingual education programs as a way for Hispanic students to preserve their language and heritage while improving academic skills. In the following viewpoint, Linda Chavez argues that the government should stop funding such programs in public schools. Bilingual education—which typically offers instruction solely in Spanish—restricts the amount of time students spend hearing and speaking English, Chavez contends, and thereby limits their future academic potential. Bilingual education programs are largely not superior to instruction in English, the author maintains. Furthermore, she asserts, most Hispanic parents would prefer state and local governments to stop forcing bilingual education on their children. Chavez is the president of the Center for Equal Opportunity in Washington, DC, and the author of *Out of the Barrio: Toward a New Politics of Hispanic Assimilation*.

As you read, consider the following questions:

1. According to the survey conducted by the Center for Equal Opportunity, what percentage of Hispanic parents would like their children to learn English as soon as possible?
2. What resources other than public schools could immigrants use to educate their children in their native language and culture, according to Chavez?

"**W**hy won't they learn English like everyone else did who came to this country?"

That's a common complaint about Hispanic immigrants, based on the perception that, unlike previous immigrants, Hispanics want to retain their native language—even insisting that their children be taught in Spanish in public schools. And indeed a huge number of Hispanic children in American public schools—perhaps as many as one million—are being taught to read and write in Spanish before they learn English. Yet most people don't realize this practice has almost nothing to do with what Hispanic parents want for their children and everything to do with government policy.

HISPANICS WANT ENGLISH EDUCATION

For more than 20 years now, politically motivated federal and state policy has dictated that Hispanic youngsters in most school districts be treated differently from other non-English-speaking students. Most Korean, Russian and Chinese immigrant children, for example, receive intensive English instruction, usually for several hours a day, in English-as-a-second-language classes. But Hispanic youngsters, many of whom were born in the U.S., are put into bilingual-education classes instead, where they are likely to hear and speak Spanish most of the day. Is this what Hispanic parents want for their children? Until now, no one cared to ask.

In August 1996, the Center for Equal Opportunity commissioned a national survey of Hispanic parents to discover what they most want their children to learn in school. A random sample of 600 parents from five cities with large Hispanic populations (Los Angeles, New York, Miami, San Antonio and Houston) participated in the telephone survey, which was conducted in both English and Spanish, depending on each respondent's preference. The results were overwhelming: Hispanic parents want their children taught English as quickly as possible. They want their children's lessons for all academic subjects taught in English, so that their children will spend more time hearing and speaking English. And they think learning to read, write and speak English is the single most important goal of education.

The survey asked Hispanic parents: "Should children of Hispanic background living in the United States be taught to read and write Spanish before they are taught English, or should they be taught English as soon as possible?" Nearly two-thirds (63%) said Hispanic students should be taught English as soon as possible, while only one-sixth (16.7%) thought they should learn Spanish first.

Yet bilingual-education advocates claim that Hispanic children must learn to read and write in Spanish first if they are to succeed in eventually mastering a second language. What's more, many bilingual programs teach not only reading and writing but also most other academic subjects first in Spanish. Nonetheless, there is little solid empirical evidence to suggest that native-language instruction is superior to all-English instruction. Researchers Christine Rossell and Keith Baker have systematically reviewed every existing bilingual-education study that meets minimal academic standards. They report that 78% of program evaluations show native-language instruction to be either no better than (45%) or actually worse than (33%) doing nothing for non-English-speaking children.

ADDITIONAL SURVEY RESULTS

When asked to choose which sentiment better reflects their opinion, 81% of Hispanic parents in our survey said "My child should be taught his/her academic courses in English, because he/she will spend more time learning English"; only 12% said "My child should be taught his/her academic courses in Spanish, even if it means he/she will spend less time learning English." Although bilingual-education advocates never present the choice this starkly, children who spend time in classrooms where Spanish is the language of instruction will necessarily spend fewer hours hearing and speaking English.

And as anyone who has ever struggled with learning a new language knows, the time spent actually practicing it is absolutely critical. In 1988 the U.S. Department of Education surveyed parents whose children were enrolled in federal programs for students with limited English and found that 78% of Mexican parents and 82% of Cuban parents opposed teaching "language minority children a non-English language if it means less time for teaching them English." Despite its own findings, the department chose not to change federal policy to reflect parents' wishes. It did not even publicize the results of the survey.

Hispanic parents in our poll ranked "learning to read, write and speak English" as their top education goal. Overall, 51% of parents surveyed ranked this first among education goals; a higher percentage of parents interviewed in Spanish (52%) than in English (45%) did so. Hispanic parents who spoke English were more likely to rank "learning other academic subjects like math, history, and science" as their highest priority (44%), compared with 19% of Spanish-speaking parents who ranked learning other academic subjects most important. Only 11% of

Should Academic courses be taught in
English or Spanish?

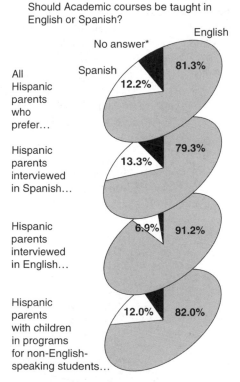

No answer*

English

Spanish

All
Hispanic
parents
who
prefer...

12.2%

81.3%

Hispanic
parents
interviewed
in Spanish...

13.3%

79.3%

Hispanic
parents
interviewed
in English...

6.9%

91.2%

Hispanic
parents
with children
in programs
for non-English-
speaking students...

12.0%

82.0%

Those who either didn't now or refused to answer

Source: Market Development Inc. survey of 600 respondents; margin of error +/− 4
percentage points.

Hispanic parents ranked "learning to read, write, and speak
Spanish" as their most important goal, and only 4% said "learning about Hispanic culture" was most important. The survey
does not suggest that learning Spanish is unimportant to Hispanic parents; rather, it simply shows that Hispanic parents
don't think that this should be a high priority for schools. Pre-
sumably, those who want to preserve their native language and
culture will do so in their homes, churches and community
groups, as have millions of previous immigrants.

STOP BLAMING HISPANICS

The Center for Equal Opportunity invites policy makers, including the Republican-controlled Congress, to study our survey re-

sults carefully. So far, Congress has avoided dealing comprehensively with bilingual-education policy, instead merely cutting funding for federal bilingual programs. But only a tiny fraction of the more than $6 billion a year spent on bilingual education nationally comes from the federal government, $178 million in fiscal year 1996. And even the proposed constitutional amendment to make English the nation's official language won't do much, if anything, to change bilingual education policy.

Twenty-three states have similar laws or constitutional provisions, including California, which funds more bilingual-education programs and forces more Hispanic students to learn their lessons in Spanish than any other state. Simply declaring English the nation's official language won't touch those programs. Real change will come only when schools start trusting parents to know what's best for their kids. It's time we stop blaming Hispanic parents for the dismal failure of bilingual education to teach their children English. The real blame belongs to federal and state officials who keep this disastrous policy in place.

| "Research shows that LEP [limited-English-proficient] students who are provided with quality bilingual education excel in their mastery of English and other subjects"

BILINGUAL EDUCATION DESERVES SUPPORT

James J. Lyons

Many people contend that bilingual education programs over-emphasize the significance of Hispanic students' native language and culture in the classroom. These critics maintain that such programs hamper students' academic progress by limiting the amount of time they hear and speak English. In the following viewpoint, James J. Lyons defends the educational merits of bilingual education. He argues that many of its opponents are motivated by a narrow-minded "English-only" political agenda that they wish to impose on education. According to Lyons, well-planned bilingual education programs are actually quite successful in helping students learn English and other academic subjects. Furthermore, he maintains, students who receive substantial bilingual education are less likely to drop out of high school and more likely to complete college. Lyons is the executive director of the National Association for Bilingual Education.

As you read, consider the following questions:

1. According to Lyons, how are Roberto Feliz's accomplishments typical of a limited-English-proficient student formerly enrolled in a bilingual education program?
2. In the author's opinion, for what two reasons do bilingual education programs remain controversial?

From James J. Lyons, "Is Bilingual Education Failing to Help America's Schoolchildren? No!" *Insight*, June 3, 1996. Reprinted by permission from *Insight*. Copyright ©1996 News World Communications, Inc. All rights reserved.

To Roberto Feliz, a Boston-area anesthesiologist, the question of whether bilingual education is failing America's schoolchildren is ridiculous. "In my schooling and learning, bilingual education was the difference between life and death," he told a congressional panel during a 1993 hearing.

A SECOND CHANCE AT EDUCATION

Feliz recounted how he "hit the wall of English" at age 10, when his family moved from the Dominican Republic to Boston. In Santo Domingo, Feliz was a straight-A student whose school nickname of "cerebrito," or "little brain," reflected his enthusiasm and accomplishments. All that changed when he was enrolled in a fifth-grade monolingual-English classroom in Boston. "Within no time the excitement that I associated with schooling turned to agonizing frustration. I can't explain how frustrating it is to know something, and know that you know it, but to be unable to communicate your knowledge in a classroom. Not only was I not learning, but teachers treated me as if I were stupid; they had no way of knowing what I knew. I hated school and would have dropped out if my mother had let me."

Feliz told lawmakers that, in his second year at Washington Irving School, a woman called Ms. Malave came to his classroom and told him that he was going to be placed in a class in which he could learn both in English and Spanish. "On that day, Ms. Malave seemed like God! And today, Ms. Malave still seems like God, for she gave me a second chance at my education." Feliz was enrolled in bilingual classes from the sixth grade until the 11th. "In the 11th grade, I found that I was truly ready to make the transition to an English-only program and made the transition successfully." He entered an honors program for the remainder of high school and won a Presidential Scholarship to Boston University. After receiving his bachelor's degree in computer science, Feliz earned a medical degree from Dartmouth University. When he appeared before the House subcommittee, he was completing the last year of a four-year residency in anesthesiology at Beth Israel Hospital, a Harvard University teaching hospital.

BILINGUAL INSTRUCTION

Feliz's experience with bilingual education is both atypical and typical of the experiences of the 2.5 million to 3.5 million "language-minority" children who speak a language other than English at home and who are deemed by state and local standards to be "limited-English-proficient," or LEP.

A 1993 Education Department report found that more than 14 percent of U.S. schools with LEP enrollments offered no special instructional services or no services specifically designed for these students, and that another 49 percent provided only monolingual English instructional services to their LEP students. More than half of the LEP students were not able to use their language and the knowledge encoded therein, as Feliz put it, to move forward in their studies.

Feliz's six-year enrollment in bilingual education also was highly atypical. The mean tenure of LEP students in bilingual education is less than three-and-a-half years, too short a period to ensure mastery of what linguists call "cognitive academic language proficiency"—the ability to learn academic content exclusively in English as well as native-English speakers. Researchers agree that it takes five to seven years for the average LEP child to meet this practical and vital measure of English proficiency. Feliz's luck in having bilingual teachers who were proficient both in English and his native language also was atypical. In 1993, nearly one of every six U.S. teachers—more than 360,000—was teaching LEP students in grades K-12. Less than half, or 42 percent, spoke the native language of their students.

Feliz's educational accomplishments, however, are typical of those LEP students who are fortunate enough to receive a substantial amount of their instruction, for a substantial period of time, through both English and their native language. Research shows that LEP students who are provided with quality bilingual education excel in their mastery of English and other subjects. At the same time, these students develop proficiency in a second language, an important resource for the nation's security and economic future.

FACILITATING LEARNING

Sixth-graders at the public Oyster Elementary School in Washington annually score at the 12th-grade level in English-language arts and at the 10th- and 11th-grade levels in math and science on nationally normed standardized achievement tests. At Oyster, all students (both native English speakers and native Spanish speakers) are taught half the time in English and half the time in Spanish in a "two-way" bilingual-education program from kindergarten through sixth grade. The fact that Feliz completed high school and went on to college also is typical of students who have received substantial bilingual education. School officials in the Calexico Unified School District, located on the U.S.-Mexico border in California, cite the availability of bilingual education as the most essential factor responsible for the district's low dropout rate and high rate of college admission. Fully 98 percent of Calexico students are Hispanic; 80 percent are LEP; and 30 percent are the children of migrant farmworkers. Average family income in Calexico, where unemployment runs between 25 and 35 percent, is less than $12,000 annually. Calexico's dropout rate of 11 to 15 percent is half the California state average for Hispanic students. In 1993, 93 percent of the district's graduating seniors were accepted by a junior college or four-year college or university. Large-scale national studies conducted and reviewed by the nation's top educational researchers confirm the success of bilingual education that makes significant use of a LEP student's native language for a substantial period of time. Both the General Accounting Office and the prestigious National Academy of Sciences have reviewed research on the effectiveness of bilingual education to answer the question of whether it is helping or harming LEP schoolchildren. Their essential findings on native-language instruction were the same:

- It does not impede and actually seems to facilitate student acquisition of English;
- It permits LEP students to make continuous and timely progress in subject-matter learning, thereby reducing the rate of student grade retention and the likelihood that students will drop out of school; and
- It results in a much higher level of parent involvement in schooling.

WHY THE CONTROVERSY?

If bilingual education is helping America's schoolchildren, why all the political fuss? There are two primary reasons. First, as with all other school programs—whether math education, science education, vocational education or special education—there are some bilingual-education programs that are not working well. Some are bilingual in name only, staffed by monolingual English-speaking teachers with no professional preparation in the instruction of LEP students. In a few instances, students have been assigned to bilingual education on the basis of an educationally irrelevant criterion such as surname, a practice condemned by the National Association for Bilingual Education, or NABE. In some localities, LEP students have been assigned to bilingual-education programs without the informed consent and choice of their parents, another practice condemned by NABE and contrary to law in federally funded programs. Yet the fact that some bilingual-education programs need improvement and reform does not warrant the elimination of native-language instruction any more than the elimination of math education, science education, vocational education or any educational program that appears to be failing some students.

A second reason bilingual education remains controversial is that a small cadre of individuals have a compelling interest in keeping it so. They have built their careers and organizations around the political cause of opposition to bilingual education.

BILINGUAL EDUCATION CAN WORK

Some bilingual programs do seem to work. Fully half of the 7,100 students in the Calexico Unified School district, in California near the Arizona state line and the Mexican border, are enrolled in bilingual classes. Most of the students are poor. But the district graduates nearly 90 percent of its high school students and sends nearly as many to four-year colleges. Calexico's curriculums for Spanish-speaking students and for English speakers are the same. The Spanish speakers move first into "sheltered English" classes conducted in both languages and then, typically within three to four years, transfer to all-English classes where they manage to perform at the same grade level as their English-speaking classmates.

William Celis, New York Times, October 15, 1995.

Linda Chavez parlayed her Hispanic surname and strident criticism of bilingual education into an appointment by President Ronald Reagan to be staff director of the U.S. Commission on Civil Rights. She later moved on to serve as president of U.S. English, a multimillion-dollar lobby founded in 1983 to oppose bilingual education and promote governmental restrictions on the use of non-English languages. Although Chavez resigned from U.S. English following press coverage of the racist views of the organization's founders and funders, she started her own organization, the Center for Equal Opportunity, to bash native-language instruction.

Chavez is aided by Larry Pratt, founder of English First, another Washington lobbying group set up exclusively to promote an English-only agenda. Pratt, who also founded and heads the lobbying organization Gun Owners of America, was the adviser to former presidential contender Pat Buchanan who resigned from the campaign after the press reported his numerous contacts with racist and extremist groups.

U.S. English funded the establishment of two "satellite" antibilingual education organizations. The first, Learning English Advocates Drive, or LEAD, was started in 1987 by a Los Angeles elementary-school teacher, Sally Peterson, who claims that "native-language-based bilingual education is a human tragedy of national proportions." Peterson teaches her LEP students exclusively in English; she is assisted by a paid bilingual paraprofessional who is able to communicate with the LEP students and their families. When Peterson was asked by the press in 1995 for information on her organization, she declined to reveal its budget, sources of funding or even the size of its membership. A second organization subsidized by U.S. English is Research in English Acquisition and Development, or READ, founded by Keith Baker, a former Education Department researcher who made a career out of attacking bilingual education. Baker's research and claims against bilingual education were reviewed by a special panel of the American Psychological Association which found them professionally substandard and invalid.

EDUCATORS SUPPORT BILINGUAL EDUCATION

The fact that virtually every national "mainstream" education organization in the United States, including the National PTA, the National School Boards Association, the Association for Supervision and Curriculum Development, Teachers of English to Speakers of Other Languages and the National Association for the Education of Young Children, supports bilingual education has not quieted criticism of bilingual instruction. That's understandable: The money from the nativist political lobbies keeps the voices of critics loud, but not loud enough to drown out the growing number of success stories such as that told by Roberto Feliz.

"Rather than promoting the best in art, the NEA continues to offer . . . the federal seal of approval to subsidize 'art' that is offensive to most Americans."

THE NATIONAL ENDOWMENT FOR THE ARTS SHOULD BE ELIMINATED

Laurence Jarvik

The National Endowment for the Arts (NEA), a government agency, was established in 1965 to promote the growth and development of the arts in the United States. The Endowment presents grants to arts agencies and nonprofit organizations for arts projects and programs. In the following viewpoint, Laurence Jarvik argues that the NEA is responsible for funding offensive, pornographic art and for promoting art with a politically correct, left-wing agenda. He maintains that the NEA should be eliminated because it is inappropriate to use government funds to promote values that many citizens find offensive. Terminating the NEA would also save federal money and eliminate the threat of government control of free expression, he concludes. Jarvik is an adjunct scholar at the Heritage Foundation, a conservative think tank.

As you read, consider the following questions:

1. According to Jarvik, how much money did the arts receive from charitable sources in 1996?
2. Who benefits the most from federal arts funding, according to the author?
3. According to Jarvik, what are some examples of pornographic films that were subsidized by the NEA?

From Laurence Jarvik, "Ten Good Reasons to Eliminate Funding for the NEA," *Backgrounder*, April 29, 1997. Reprinted by permission of The Heritage Foundation.

As the U.S. Congress struggles to balance the federal budget and end the decades-long spiral of deficit spending, few programs seem more worthy of outright elimination than the National Endowment for the Arts (NEA). Indeed, since its inception in 1965, few federal agencies have been mired in more controversy than the NEA. Nevertheless, steadfast partisans of "welfare for artists" continue to defend the Endowment, asserting that it promotes philanthropic giving, makes cultural programs accessible to those who can least afford them, and protects America's cultural heritage.

In fact, the NEA is an unwarranted extension of the federal government into the voluntary sector. The Endowment, furthermore, does not promote charitable giving. Despite Endowment claims that its efforts bring art to the inner city, the agency offers little more than a direct subsidy to the cultured, upper-middle class. Finally, rather than promoting the best in art, the NEA continues to offer tax dollars and the federal seal of approval to subsidize "art" that is offensive to most Americans.

THE NEA SHOULD BE DEFUNDED

There are several good reasons to eliminate funding for the NEA:

• *The arts will have more than enough support without the NEA.* The arts were flowering before the NEA came into being in 1965. Indeed, the Endowment was created partly because of the tremendous popular appeal of the arts at the time. Alvin Toffler's *The Culture Consumers*, published in 1964, surveyed the booming audience for art in the United States, a side benefit of a growing economy and low inflation. Toffler's book recalls the arts prior to the creation of the NEA—the era of the great George Balanchine and Agnes de Mille ballets, for example, when 26 million viewers would turn to CBS broadcasts of Leonard Bernstein and the New York Philharmonic. In fact, nearly all of the major orchestras in the United States existed before 1965, and will continue to exist after NEA subsidies are ended.

In spite of the vast splendor created by American artists prior to 1965, partisans of the NEA claim that the arts in the United States would face almost certain demise should the Endowment be abolished. Yet Endowment funding is just a drop in the bucket compared to giving to the arts by private citizens. For example, in 1996, the Metropolitan Opera of New York received $390,000 from the Endowment, a federal subsidy that totals only 0.29 percent of the Opera's annual income of $133 million—and amounts to less than the ticket revenue for a single sold-out performance.

The growth of private-sector charitable giving in recent years has rendered NEA funding relatively insignificant to the arts community. Overall giving to the arts in 1996 totaled almost $10 billion—up from $6.5 billion in 1991—dwarfing the NEA's federal subsidy. This 40 percent increase in private giving occurred during the same period that the NEA budget was reduced by 40 percent from approximately $170 million to $99.5 million. Thus, as conservatives had predicted, cutting the federal NEA subsidy coincided with increased private support for the arts and culture. . . .

• *The NEA is welfare for cultural elitists.* Despite Endowment claims that federal funding permits underprivileged individuals to gain access to the arts, NEA grants offer little more than a subsidy to the well-to-do. One-fifth of direct NEA grants go to multimillion-dollar arts organizations. Harvard University Political Scientist Edward C. Banfield has noted that the "art public is now, as it has always been, overwhelmingly middle and upper middle class and above average in income—relatively prosperous people who would probably enjoy art about as much in the absence of subsidies." The poor and the middle class, thus, benefit less from public art subsidies than does the museum- and orchestra-going upper-middle class. British economist David Sawers argues that "those who finance the subsidies through taxes are likely to be different from and poorer than those who benefit from the subsidies." In fact, the $99.5 million that funds the NEA also represents the entire annual tax burden for over 436,000 working-class American families. . . .

GRANTS FOR OFFENSIVE ART?

• *The NEA will continue to fund pornography.* On March 6, 1997, Congressman Pete Hoekstra (R-MI), Chairman of the Education and Workforce Subcommittee that has oversight over the NEA, complained about books published by an NEA-funded press called "Fiction Collective 2," which he described as an "offense to the senses." Hoekstra cited four Fiction Collective 2 books and noted that the publisher's parent organization had received an additional $45,000 grant to establish a World Wide Web site. According to *The Washington Times,* the NEA granted $25,000 to Fiction Collective 2, which featured works containing sexual torture, incest, child sex, and sadomasochism; the "excerpts depict a scene in which a brother-sister team rape their younger sister, the torture of a Mexican male prostitute and oral sex between two women." Pat Trueman, former Chief of the Child Exploitation and Obscenity Section of the United States Department of Justice Criminal Division, characterized the works as "troubling" and said the NEA posed a "direct threat to the prosecution" of obscenity and child pornography because of its official stamp on such material. Incredibly, the NEA continues to defend such funding decisions publicly. "Fiction Collective 2 is a highly respected, pre-eminent publisher of innovative, quality fiction," NEA spokeswoman Cherie Simon said.

The current controversy is nothing new for the NEA. In November 1996, Representative Hoekstra questioned NEA funding of a film distributor handling "patently offensive and possibly pornographic movies—several of which appear to deal with the sexuality of children." He noted the NEA gave $112,700 over three years to "Women Make Movies," which subsidized distribution of films including:

- "Ten Cents a Dance," a three-vignette video in which "two women awkwardly discuss their mutual attraction." It "depicts anonymous bathroom sex between two men" and includes an "ironic episode of heterosexual phone sex."
- "Sex Fish" portrays a "furious montage of oral sex, public rest-room cruising and . . . tropical fish," the catalog says.
- "Coming Home" talks of the "sexy fun of trying to fit a lesbian couple in a bathtub!"

- "Seventeen Rooms" purports to answer the question, "What do lesbians do in bed?"
- "BloodSisters" reveals a "diverse cross-section of the lesbian [sadomasochistic] community."

Three other films center on the sexual or lesbian experiences of girls age 12 and under. "These listings have the appearance of a veritable taxpayer-funded peep show," said Hoekstra in a letter to NEA Chairman Alexander. He noted that the distributor was circulating films of Annie Sprinkle, a pornographic "performance artist" who appeared at "The Kitchen," a New York venue receiving NEA support. In response, *The New York Times* launched an *ad hominem* attack on Hoekstra (while neglecting to mention that *The New York Times* Company Foundation had sponsored Sprinkle's performance at one time).

Another frequent response supporters of the NEA make to such criticism is to claim that instances of funding pornography and other indecent material were simple mistakes. But such "mistakes" seem part of a regular pattern of support for indecency, repeated year after year. . . .

POLITICAL CORRECTNESS AND MULTICULTURALISM

- *The NEA promotes politically correct art.* A radical virus of multiculturalism, moreover, has permanently infected the agency, causing artistic efforts to be evaluated by race, ethnicity, and sexual orientation instead of artistic merit. In 1993, Roger Kimball reported that an "effort to impose quotas and politically correct thinking" was "taking precedence over mundane considerations of quality." Perhaps the most prominent case of reverse discrimination was the cancellation of a grant to the *Hudson Review*, which based its selections on "literary merit."

More recently, Jan Breslauer wrote in *The Washington Post* that multiculturalism was now "systemic" at the agency. Breslauer, theater critic for the *Los Angeles Times*, pointed out that "private grantees are required to conform to the NEA's specifications" and the "art world's version of affirmative action" has had "a profoundly corrosive effect on the American arts—pigeonholing artists and pressuring them to produce work that satisfies a politically correct agenda rather than their best creative instincts." NEA funding of "race-based politics" has encouraged ethnic separatism and Balkanization at the expense of a shared American culture. Because of federal dollars, Breslauer discovered, "Artists were routinely placed on bills, in seasons, or in exhibits because of who they were rather than what kind of art they'd made" and "artistic directors began to push artists towar 'purer' (read: stereotypical) expressions of the ethnicity they were paying them to represent." The result, Breslauer concluded, is that "most people in the arts establishment continue to defer, at least publicly, to the demands of political correctness."

Aside from such blatant cultural engineering, the NEA also seems intent on pushing "art" that offers little more than a decidedly left-wing agenda:

* In the summer of 1996, the Phoenix Art Museum, a recipient of NEA funding, presented an exhibit featuring: an American flag in a toilet, an American flag made out of human skin, and a flag on the museum floor to be stepped upon. Fabian Montoya, an 11-year-old boy, picked up the American flag to rescue it. Museum curators replaced it, prompting Representative Matt Salmon (R-AZ) and the Phoenix American Legion to applaud the boy's patriotism by presenting him with a flag that had flown over the U.S. Capitol. Whereas the American Legion, (then) Senator Bob Dole, and House Speaker Newt Gingrich condemned the exhibit, NEA Chairman Alexander remained conspicuously silent.

* Artist Robbie Conal plastered "NEWTWIT" posters all over Washington, D.C., and sold them at the NEA-subsidized Washington Project for the Arts. . . .

AN INABILITY TO CHANGE

* *The NEA is beyond reform.* Recent history shows that despite cosmetic "reorganizations" at the NEA, the Endowment is impervious to genuine change because of the specific arts constituencies it serves. Every few years, whether it be by Nancy Hanks in the Nixon Administration, Livingston Biddle in the Carter Administration, or Frank Hodsoll in the Reagan Administration, NEA administrators promise that reorganization will bring massive change to the agency. All these efforts have failed. It was, in fact, under Mr. Hodsoll's tenure in the Reagan Administration that grants were awarded to Robert Mapplethorpe, known for his homoerotic photography, and to Andres Serrano, infamous for creating the exhibit "Piss Christ.". . .

ARTS FUNDING THREATENS DEMOCRATIC PRINCIPLES

* *Funding the NEA disturbs the U.S. tradition of limited government.* In retrospect, turmoil over the NEA was predictable, due to the long tradition in the United States of opposing the use of federal tax dollars to fund the arts. During the Constitutional Convention in Philadelphia in 1787, delegate Charles Pinckney introduced a motion calling for the federal government to subsidize the arts

in the United States. Although the Founding Fathers were cultured men who knew firsthand of various European systems for public arts patronage, they overwhelmingly rejected Pinckney's suggestion because of their belief in limited, constitutional government. Accordingly, nowhere in its list of powers enumerated and delegated to the federal government does the Constitution specify a power to subsidize the arts.

Moreover, as David Boaz of the Cato Institute argues, federal arts subsidies pose the danger of federal control over expression: "Government funding of anything involves government control. . . . As we should not want an established church, so we should not want established art." As economist Tyler Cowen notes, "When the government promotes its favored art, the most innovative creators find it more difficult to rise to the top. . . . But the true costs of government funding do not show up on our tax bill. The NEA and other government arts agencies politicize art and jeopardize the principles of democratic government." The French government, for example, tried to suppress Impressionism through its control of the French Academy of Arts.

The deep-seated American belief against public support of artists continues today. Public opinion polls, moreover, show that a majority of Americans favor elimination of the NEA when the agency is mentioned by name. A June 1995 *Wall Street Journal*–Peter Hart poll showed 54 percent of Americans favored eliminating the NEA entirely versus 38 percent in favor of maintaining it at any level of funding. An earlier January 19, 1995, *Los Angeles Times* poll found 69 percent of the American people favored cutting the NEA budget. More recently, a poll performed by The Polling Company in March 1997 demonstrated that 57 percent of Americans favor the proposition that "Congress should stop funding the NEA with federal taxpayer dollars and instead leave funding decisions with state government and private groups."

TERMINATE THE NEA

After more than three decades, the National Endowment for the Arts has failed in its mission to enhance cultural life in the United States. Despite numerous attempts to reinvent it, the NEA continues to promote the worst excesses of multiculturalism and political correctness, subsidizing art that demeans the values of ordinary Americans. As the federal debt soars to over $5 trillion, it is time to terminate the NEA as a wasteful, unjustified, unnecessary, and unpopular federal expenditure.

Ending the NEA would be good for the arts and good for America.

"[The Arts Endowment has given] new emphasis and vitality to American creativity and scholarship, and to the cultural achievements that are among America's greatest strengths."

THE NATIONAL ENDOWMENT FOR THE ARTS SHOULD BE RETAINED

Edward Kennedy

In the following viewpoint, Edward Kennedy argues in favor of the National Endowment for the Arts, a government agency that subsidizes artists and nonprofit arts organizations. Kennedy contends that federal arts funding—which is supported by Democrats, Republicans, and the general public—ensures that all Americans have access to the arts. Furthermore, he maintains, the right-wing argument that the NEA should be eliminated because it has funded offensive art is misleading. Only a small fraction of NEA grants have subsidized inappropriate material, the author points out, and critics have tried to use this material to justify eliminating the agency. In actuality, he asserts, the NEA provides necessary funding for many successful and innovative arts projects that enrich American culture. Kennedy is a Democratic senator from Massachusetts.

As you read, consider the following questions:

1. According to Kennedy, how many NEA grants have raised serious concerns about the funding of inappropriate material?
2. What is the stated mission of the NEA, according to the author?
3. According to Kennedy, how does arts education affect learning potential?

Reprinted from a press release from the office of Edward M. Kennedy, September 17, 1997.

Here we go again. Every year since 1989, Congress has held a highly charged debate about the future of the National Endowment for the Arts. 1997 is no different. Ironically, extremists opposing the NEA have recently been claiming that there has been inadequate oversight of the agency. Dollar for dollar, it is likely that no agency has been more heavily scrutinized than the Arts Endowment.

The arts and humanities have, and deserve to have, a central role in the life of America. The Arts Endowment has contributed immensely to that role. It has encouraged the growth and development of the arts in communities across the nation, giving new emphasis and vitality to American creativity and scholarship, and to the cultural achievements that are among America's greatest strengths.

Americans have a great deal to celebrate and learn about our extraordinary cultural traditions. The arts are an important part of our complex and modern society, and will play a key role in fulfilling our country's many possibilities for the future.

CRITICISMS OF THE ENDOWMENT

Critics used to claim that the Endowment spent money unwisely—awarding grants to unqualified artists or to artists that clearly did not merit federal aid. But the critics quickly ran out of examples. Over the period of its entire 32-year history, a grand total of about 25 of the tens of thousands of grants awarded by the Endowment have raised genuine concerns. Yet, the budget for the Arts Endowment has been cut to penalize the agency for these so-called inappropriate grants. Other restrictions have also been imposed—on content, on seasonal support grants, on grants to individuals, and on subgrants.

Nothing will ever satisfy the critics, because their real intent is to eliminate any Federal role in the arts. Their goal is to abolish the agency—either directly by denying it any funds at all, or, indirectly by block-granting all the funds to the states.

In fact, the Arts Endowment has an extraordinary record of successful achievement. As a result of the its leadership over the past three decades, there are now double the number of orchestras in America, eleven times the number of dance companies, and fifty times the number of local arts agencies. The NEA reaches out to thousands of America's communities and neighborhoods. It is functioning as it should, encouraging the arts in all parts of the country, providing the seed money that enables local arts to grow and thrive.

Let's be honest. In recent years, since the right wing's misguided ideological assault on the agency first began, Congress has gone the extra mile. We have taken every reasonable action to ensure that the Arts Endowment only supports grants and programs that are responsible, that fulfill the agency's widely accepted mission, and that reach the widest possible audience. Every year, the agency has to run the appropriations gauntlet, and every year, it convinces a majority of Congress that it deserves support. 1997 should be no different, because there is no new evidence to justify the critics' shameful attack. . . .

THE NEA MAKES A DIFFERENCE

The agency has made a significant contribution to the quality of life in thousands of communities in our country. The arts have broad appeal, and the Endowment's mission is to encourage artists and institutions across the country to create, produce and present programs to tap and encourage that appeal. In 1996, for example, the NEA supported significant programs such as the Delaware Theater Company, the Atlanta Ballet, the Tulsa Philharmonic Society, the University of Southern Mississippi's Folk and Traditional Arts program, and the International Association of Jazz Educators.

Countless other examples can be cited. Federal support for the arts has clearly made a large difference in communities across the country. The current federal role is significant, and it has overwhelming support in every state. Families want their children to visit symphonies and museums. They want to enjoy theater and dance. The arts are more than a diversion or entertainment. They are educational and enriching, and their central place in the nation's life and experiences should be supported and increased.

The Conference of Mayors has strongly endorsed the Arts Endowment. These local officials, who know their communities best, clearly understand the positive role of the arts. They know that the arts contribute to the vitality of their locality, and increase its economic base as well.

In Massachusetts, the arts community is thriving and dynamic. A wealth of cultural and educational activities is available to every citizen. These activities also attract tourists to Massachusetts. Recently, the Museum of Science presented its hugely successful "Leonardo da Vinci" exhibition. A major retrospective on Picasso's early years is about to open at the Museum of Fine Arts. Many of my colleagues, I am sure, had the opportunity to see this extraordinary exhibition at the National Gallery of Art in

Washington. The Endowment's support helped to make this dramatic exhibition possible.

People in every state treasure their own arts institutions and arts programs in the same way. Whatever the size of the state or community, the impact of the arts is significant and indisputable, from the youngest child to the oldest senior citizen.

THE NEED FOR FEDERAL SUPPORT

Leaders in state and local institutions across the country are convinced that support by the Arts Endowment has been a significant part of their success. Federal aid is seed money. It has never been intended to replace state or local or private support for the arts. But it has often been a critical component in the overall development and success of countless local institutions.

A CAMPAIGN OF MISINFORMATION

Here in the United States the principal of government support for the arts and culture has had broad bi-partisan backing for more than three decades. Democrats and Republicans have worked together to make the experience of the arts accessible to everyone, including Americans who do not live in or near our large, urban cultural centers. . . .

In recent years, however, . . . [some] politicians and political groups have decided to hold up for ridicule a few artists and a few works of art and they have tried to use that ridicule to diminish public support for the arts as a whole. In their attempt to market their belief, that government should stay out of arts and ideas, they have engaged in a profoundly disingenuous campaign of misinformation and myth-making.

Alec Baldwin, Briefing at the National Press Club in Washington, DC, March 10, 1997.

In many communities, the federal role has been indispensable, especially in disseminating innovative programs to institutions that might not have the resources to develop and produce their own programs.

Arts education is an excellent example of this impact. Music is an especially effective tool in developing the discipline and the learning potential of students. Recent studies by the College Board show that students who have studied four years of music or more do significantly better in both their math and verbal scores on standard SAT tests.

We should be doing more, not less, for the arts. The heavy-handed attempt by the House Republican leadership to eliminate the Arts Endowment should be categorically rejected, and it is gratifying that President Clinton has pledged to veto any bill that reaches his desk that attempts to do so. In fact, many of the agency's strongest and most effective supporters are on the Republican side of the aisle.

Congress should start listening to the people and stop bashing this small agency. When we listen to the exaggerated protests of the critics, it is hard to remember that we are talking about a program that costs each taxpayer 37 cents a year.

We have already taken a full range of steps to see that the agency operates as effectively and responsibly as possible. It is time to support fair funding for this important agency, and give it the solid vote of confidence it deserves.

TIMELESS GOALS

President John Kennedy, in his 1960 campaign for President, discussed the close historical relationship between great achievement in public life and great achievement in the arts. He said, "There is a connection, hard to explain logically but easy to feel, between achievement in public life and progress in the arts. The age of Pericles was also the age of Phidias. The age of Lorenzo de Medici was also the age of Leonardo da Vinci. The age of Elizabeth also the age of Shakespeare. And the New Frontier for which I campaign in public life, can also be a new frontier for American art."

Three years later, as President, in a major address at Amherst College in October 1963, he said this: "I look forward to an America which will reward achievement in the arts as we reward achievement in business or statecraft. I look forward to an America which will steadily raise the standard of artistic accomplishment and which will steadily enlarge cultural opportunities for all our citizens. And I look forward to an America which commands respect throughout the world not only for its strength but for its civilization as well."

Those are timeless goals, they apply to our own day and generation as well. I urge the Senate to heed them, to give the arts in America the strong support they so eminently deserve.

PERIODICAL BIBLIOGRAPHY

The following articles have been selected to supplement the diverse views presented in this chapter. Addresses are provided for periodicals not indexed in the *Readers' Guide to Periodical Literature*, the *Alternative Press Index*, the *Social Sciences Index*, or the *Index to Legal Periodicals and Books*.

Jorge Amselle	"Adios, Bilingual Ed," *Policy Review*, November/December 1997.
Christopher Caldwell	"Art for Politics' Sake," *Commentary*, February 1998.
Allan Carlson	"Twenty-Five Years into the Culture of Death," *Vital Speeches of the Day*, March 15, 1998.
Christianity Today	"Our Selective Rage," August 12, 1996.
Edd Doerr	"Church and State: *Roe*, a Best Seller, and PK," *Humanist*, January/February 1998.
Norine Dworkin	"The Abortion Issue: There Is No 'Choice' Without Providers," *On the Issues*, Fall 1993.
Faye Fiore	"On Fifty Years of Fighting for Arts Funding in America," *Los Angeles Times*, September 14, 1997.
Robert Freeman	"How to Save the NEA," *Wall Street Journal*, November 28, 1997.
James K. Galbraith	"English Über Alles," *Nation*, September 29, 1997.
Martin Garbus	"The Indecent Standard," *Nation*, April 13, 1998.
Bruce Handy	"Where the Elite Meet to Be Aesthetes," *Time*, November 3, 1997.
Frederica Mathewes-Green	"We Can Find Common Ground on Abortion," *U.S. Catholic*, January 1998.
Gregory Rodriguez	"English Lesson in California," *Nation*, April 20, 1998.
Ron K. Unz	"Bilingual Is a Damaging Myth," *Los Angeles Times*, October 19, 1997.
Naomi Wolf	"Our Bodies, Our Souls," *New Republic*, October 16, 1995.

FOR FURTHER DISCUSSION

CHAPTER 1

1. James Davison Hunter maintains that America's culture wars reflect a deep division in public opinion over controversial social issues. Rhys H. Williams contends that such a division is more characteristic of activists and policymakers than of the general public. Evaluate each author's opinion, then formulate your own argument describing the nature of America's culture wars.

2. Virginia Ramey Mollenkott argues that Christian fundamentalists and several right-wing organizations have intensified cultural conflict in the United States. Scott M. Morris, however, contends that cultural discord has resulted from secular society's misinterpretations of religious people's motivations. Which viewpoint do you agree with, and why?

CHAPTER 2

1. George Roche argues that a loss of traditional moral values has resulted in America's cultural decline. Charles Lindholm and John A. Hall maintain that voluntary cooperation among Americans has maintained the country's social order. In each viewpoint, try to find two supporting arguments that you personally agree with. Why do you agree with them?

2. Cal Thomas asserts that the upheavals of the 1960s harmed American culture, while Terry H. Anderson contends that the 1960s made America more tolerant and egalitarian. What evidence does each author present to support his conclusion? Whose use of evidence is more persuasive? Explain your answer.

3. Compare John Leo's and Ben J. Wattenburg's arguments about the quality of America's popular culture. On what points do these two authors agree? On what points do they disagree?

4. Martin L. Gross maintains that political correctness is a harmful social movement that is crippling American culture. What examples does he use to support his argument? Does John K. Wilson's viewpoint effectively refute Gross's examples? Why or why not?

CHAPTER 3

1. John M. Frame contends that belief in God is necessary for morality. Theodore Schick Jr. maintains that morality does not require belief in a supreme being. In your opinion, which of

these authors presents a stronger case? Explain your answer, using examples from the viewpoints.

2. Ralph Reed argues that the promotion of religious conservatism would benefit American politics and culture. Conversely, Amy Waldman contends that a revitalized religious liberalism would strengthen American society. How do the arguments of these two authors reflect differing views on the role of Judeo-Christian principles in American politics? Whose argument do you find more persuasive?

3. Hedy Nai-Lin Chang defines multiculturalism as a value system that can unify diverse groups of people by cultivating respect for cultural, ethnic, and linguistic differences. Linda Chavez maintains that multiculturalism creates enmity among groups by focusing on racial and ethnic differences rather than on unifying values and principles. In your opinion, which author's definition of multiculturalism is more accurate? Use evidence from the viewpoints to support your answer.

CHAPTER 4

1. For different reasons, the *Progressive* and *National Review* conclude that the twenty-fifth anniversary of *Roe v. Wade* was not a cause for celebration. Compare the *Progressive*'s contention that government has infringed on women's right to abortion with *National Review*'s argument that the government has sanctioned an increasing disrespect for life. Which viewpoint do you agree with? Explain your answer using evidence from each viewpoint.

2. Linda Chavez cites survey research and statistics to help support her contention that the government should stop backing bilingual-education programs. James J. Lyons uses an extended anecdotal example to bolster his argument in favor of bilingual education. Which author's technique do you find more compelling? Why?

3. Laurence Jarvik contends that the National Endowment for the Arts (NEA) should be eliminated, while Edward Kennedy argues in the support of the NEA. Jarvik is affiliated with the Heritage Foundation, a conservative think tank; Kennedy is a liberal Democratic senator. Does knowing their backgrounds influence your assessment of their arguments? Explain your answer.

ORGANIZATIONS TO CONTACT

The editors have compiled the following list of organizations concerned with the issues debated in this book. The descriptions are derived from materials provided by the organizations. All have publications or information available for interested readers. The list was compiled on the date of publication of the present volume; the information provided here may change. Be aware that many organizations take several weeks or longer to respond to inquiries, so allow as much time as possible.

American Center for Law and Justice (ACLJ)
PO Box 64429, Virginia Beach, VA 23467
(757) 226-2489 • fax: (757) 226-2836
e-mail: aclj@exis.net • website: http://www.aclj.org
The center is a public interest law firm and educational organization dedicated to promoting liberty, life, and the family. ACLJ provides legal services and support to attorneys and others who are involved in defending the religious and civil liberties of Americans. It publishes the booklets *Students' Rights and the Public Schools* and *Taking the Gospel to the Streets: Your Rights to Preach the Good News in Public Places.*

American Civil Liberties Union (ACLU)
132 W. 43rd St., New York, NY 10036
(212) 944-9800 • fax: (212) 869-9065
e-mail: aclu@aclu.org • website: http://www.aclu.org
The ACLU is a national organization that works to defend Americans' civil rights guaranteed in the U.S. Constitution. The ACLU publishes the semiannual newsletter *Civil Liberties Alert* as well as the handbook *The Right to Religious Liberty* and the briefing paper "Artistic Freedom."

Americans United for Separation of Church and State (AU)
1816 Jefferson Pl. NW, Washington, DC 20036
(202) 466-3234 • fax: (202) 466-2587
e-mail: americansunited@au.org • website: http://www.au.org
AU works to protect the constitutional principle of church-state separation. It opposes mandatory prayer in public schools, tax dollars for parochial schools, and religious groups' participating in politics. AU publishes the monthly *Church & State* magazine as well as issue papers, legislative alerts, reference materials, and books.

Center for the Study of Popular Culture
PO Box 67398, Los Angeles, CA 90067
(310) 843-3699 • fax: (310) 843-3692
e-mail: brdonaldson@cspc.org
websites: http://www.cspc.org • http://www.frontpagemag.com
This educational center offers legal assistance and addresses many topics, including political correctness, cultural diversity, and discrimina-

tion. Its civil rights project provides legal assistance to citizens challenging affirmative action and promotes equal opportunity for all individuals. The center publishes the magazine *Heterodoxy* and the on-line *FrontPage* magazine.

Center for the Study of White American Culture
245 W. Fourth Ave., Roselle, NJ 07203
(908) 241-5439
e-mail: contact@euroamerican.org
website: http://www.euroamerican.org

The center is a multiracial organization that supports cultural exploration and self-discovery among white Americans. It also encourages dialogue among all racial and cultural groups concerning the role of white American culture in the larger American society. It publishes a quarterly newsletter and the Whiteness Papers series, including "Decentering Whiteness" and "White Men and the Denial of Racism."

Council for Secular Humanism
PO Box 664, Amherst, NY 14226-0664
(716) 636-7571 • fax: (716) 636-1733
e-mail: info@SecularHumanism.org
website: http://www.secularhumanism.org

The council is an educational organization dedicated to fostering the growth of democracy, secular humanism, and the principles of free inquiry. It publishes the magazine *Free Inquiry* as well as papers in the Secular Humanist Viewpoints series, such as "Are the Ten Commandments Relevant Today?"

Fairness and Accuracy in Reporting (FAIR)
130 W. 25th St., New York, NY 10001
(212) 633-6700 • fax: (212) 727-7668
e-mail: fair@fair.org • website: http://www.fair.org

FAIR is a national media watch group that investigates conservative bias in news coverage. Its members advocate greater diversity in the press and believe that structural reform is needed to break up the dominant media conglomerates and establish alternative, independent sources of information. *Extra!* is FAIR's bimonthly magazine of media criticism.

Family Research Council
801 G St. NW, Washington, DC, 20001
(202) 393-2100 • fax: (202) 393-2134
website: http://www.frc.org

The council is a conservative research, resource, and educational organization that promotes the traditional family. The council advocates religious liberty and opposes abortion and federal funding of the arts. It publishes *Culture Facts*, a weekly newsletter.

Freedom from Religion Foundation, Inc.
PO Box 750, Madison, WI 53701
(608) 256-8900
website: http://www.infidels.org/org/ffrf
The foundation works to keep state and church separate and to educate the public about the views of nontheists. It publishes the newspaper *Freethought Today* ten times per year.

The Heritage Foundation
214 Massachusetts Ave. NE, Washington, DC 20002-4999
(800) 544-4843 • (202) 546-4400 • fax: (202) 544-6979
e-mail: pubs@heritage.org • website: http://www.heritage.org
The foundation is a public policy research institute that advocates limited government, individual freedom, and traditional values. Its many publications include the position papers "Freedom and Responsibility: The Role Values Play in Shaping Public Policy," "Why Religion Matters: The Importance of Religious Practice on Social Stability," and "Ten Good Reasons to Eliminate Funding for the National Endowment for the Arts."

Interfaith Alliance
1012 14th St. NW, Washington, DC 20005
(202) 639-6370 • (202) 639-6375
e-mail: tia@tialliance.org • website: http://www.tialliance.org
The alliance is a nonpartisan organization that advances a mainstream, faith-based political agenda. Its members promote religion as a healing and constructive force in public life and oppose the extreme values of the religious right. It publishes the *Light*, a quarterly newsletter.

Media Research Center
113 S. West St., Suite 200, Alexandria, VA 22314
(800) 672-1423 • (703)683-9733 • fax: (703) 683-9736
e-mail: mrc@mediaresearch.org
website: http://www.mediaresearch.org

The center is a media watch group that monitors liberal bias in the media. Its programs include the Parents Television Council, which advocates family programming, and its news division, which monitors liberal bias in news coverage. Its publications include the newsletter *MediaWatch* and the report *Faith in a Box: Entertainment Television on Religion—1997*.

National Campaign for Freedom of Expression (NCFE)
918 F St. NW, #609, Washington, DC 20004
(202) 393-2787 • fax: (202) 347-7376
e-mail: ncfe@artswire.org • website: http://www.artswire.org/ncfe
NCFE is an educational and advocacy network of artists, arts organizations, and concerned citizens who work to protect and extend freedom of artistic expression and fight censorship throughout the United States. It publishes the books *The Cultural Battlefield: Art Censorship and Public*

Funding and Artistic Freedom Handbook: A Guide to Understanding, Preparing for, and Responding to Challenges to Your Freedom of Artistic Expression.

National Coalition Against Censorship
275 Seventh Ave., New York, NY 10001
(212) 807-6222 • fax: (212) 807-6245
e-mail: ncac@ncac.org • website: http://www.ncac.org

The coalition represents more than forty national organizations that strive to end suppression of free speech and the press. It publishes the quarterly *Censorship News*.

National Endowment for the Arts (NEA)
1100 Pennsylvania Ave. NW, Washington, DC 20506
(202) 682-5400 • fax: (202) 682-5611
website: http://arts.endow.gov

The endowment is a federal government agency charged with supporting the arts in America. Through grants, leadership initiatives, and partnerships with public and private organizations, the NEA seeks to foster the excellence, diversity, and vitality of the arts and to broaden public access to them. Its publications include *Understanding How the Arts Contribute to Excellent Education* and the *American Canvas* report, an analysis and examination of the state of the nonprofit arts in America.

People for the American Way Foundation
2000 M St. NW, Suite 400, Washington, DC 20036
e-mail: pfaw@pfaw.org • website: http://www.pfaw.org

People for the American Way Foundation is a nonprofit, nonpartisan organization that opposes the political agenda of the religious right. Through public education, lobbying, and legal advocacy the foundation defends free expression in the arts, works for equal rights for gays and lesbians, and supports public schools. The foundation publishes the reports *Artistic Freedom Under Attack, A Right Wing and a Prayer: The Religious Right and Your Public Schools*, and *"Parental Rights": The Trojan Horse of the Religious Right Attack on Public Education*.

U.S. Department of Education
Office of Bilingual Education and Minority Languages Affairs
600 Independence Ave. SW, Washington, DC 20202-6510
e-mail: askncbe@ncbe.gwu.edu
website: http://www.ed.gov/offices/obemla

The office helps school districts meet their responsibility to provide equal education opportunity to children who are not proficient in English. It publishes fact sheets, policy statements, and reports on bilingual education.

BIBLIOGRAPHY OF BOOKS

Terry H. Anderson   *The Movement and the Sixties.* Oxford, NY: Oxford University Press, 1995.

Robert M. Baird and Stuart E. Rosenbaum, eds.   *The Ethics of Abortion: Pro-Life vs. Pro-Choice.* Rev. ed. Buffalo: Prometheus Books, 1993.

Chip Berlet, ed.   *Eyes Right! Challenging the Right Wing Backlash.* Boston: South End Press, 1995.

Richard Bernstein   *Dictatorship of Virtue: Multiculturalism and the Battle for America's Future.* New York: Alfred A. Knopf, 1994.

Robert Bly   *The Sibling Society.* Reading, MA: Addison-Wesley, 1996.

Robert H. Bork   *Slouching Towards Gomorrah: Modern Liberalism and American Decline.* New York: HarperCollins, 1996.

Robert Boston   *The Most Dangerous Man in America: Pat Robertson and the Rise of the Christian Coalition.* Amherst, NY: Prometheus Books, 1996.

Stephen L. Carter   *Civility: Manners, Morals, and the Etiquette of Democracy.* New York: BasicBooks, 1998.

Lynne V. Cheney   *Telling the Truth: Why Our Culture and Our Country Have Stopped Making Sense—and What We Can Do About It.* New York: Simon & Schuster, 1995.

Ron Chepesiuk   *Sixties Radicals, Then and Now: Candid Conversations with Those Who Shaped the Era.* Jefferson, NC: McFarland, 1995.

George E. Curry, ed.   *The Affirmative Action Debate.* Reading, MA: Addison-Wesley, 1996.

Kenneth Dyson and Walter Homolka, eds.   *Culture First! Promoting Standards in the New Media Age.* London: Cassell, 1996.

John M. Ellis   *Literature Lost: Social Agendas and the Corruption of the Humanities.* New Haven, CT: Yale University Press, 1997.

Richard Feldstein   *Political Correctness: A Response from the Cultural Left.* Minneapolis: University of Minnesota Press, 1997.

Thomas Frank   *The Conquest of Cool.* Chicago: University of Chicago Press, 1997.

Marilyn Friedman and Jan Narveson   *Political Correctness: For and Against.* Lanham, MD: Rowman & Littlefield, 1995.

Marjorie Garber   *Symptoms of Culture.* New York: Routledge, 1998.

Todd Gitlin	*The Twilight of Common Dreams: Why America Is Wracked by Culture Wars.* New York: Henry Holt, 1995.
Nathan Glazer	*We Are All Multiculturalists Now.* Cambridge, MA: Harvard University Press, 1997.
Cynthia Gorney	*Articles of Faith: A Frontline History of the Abortion Wars.* New York: Simon & Schuster, 1998.
David Hollinger	*Postethnic America: Beyond Multiculturalism.* New York: BasicBooks, 1995.
bell hooks	*Outlaw Culture: Resisting Representations.* New York: Routledge, 1994.
Susan Huck	*Why Do We Americans Submit to This?* McLean, VA: Newcomb, 1997.
Robert Hughes	*Culture of Complaint: The Fraying of America.* New York: Oxford University Press, 1993.
James Davison Hunter	*Before the Shooting Begins: Searcing for Democracy in America's Culture War.* New York: Free Press, 1994.
James Davison Hunter	*Culture Wars: The Struggle to Define America.* New York: BasicBooks, 1991.
Peter Kreeft	*Ecumenical Jihad: Ecumenism and the Culture War.* San Francisco: Ignatius Press, 1996.
John Leonard	*Smoke and Mirrors: Violence, Television, and Other American Cultures.* New York: New Press, 1997.
Michael Lerner	*The Politics of Meaning: Restoring Hope and Possibility in an Age of Cynicism.* Reading, MA: Addison-Wesley, 1996.
Charles Lyons	*The New Censors: Movies and the Culture Wars.* Philadelphia: Temple University Press, 1997.
William Martin	*With God on Our Side: The Rise of the Religious Right in America.* New York: Broadway Books, 1996.
Gary B. Nash, Charlotte Crabtree, and Ross E. Dunn	*History on Trial: Culture Wars and the Teaching of the Past.* New York: Alfred A. Knopf, 1997.
James L. Nolan Jr.	*The American Culture Wars: Current Contests and Future Prospects.* Charlottesville: University Press of Virginia, 1996.
Ralph Reed	*Active Faith: How Christians Are Changing the Soul of America.* New York: Free Press, 1996.
James Risen and Judy L. Thomas	*Wrath of Angels: The American Abortion War.* New York: BasicBooks, 1998.
Robert Royal, ed.	*Reinventing the American People: Unity and Diversity Today.* Grand Rapids: Eerdemans, 1995.

Alvin J. Schmidt	*The Menace of Multiculturalism.* Westport, CT: Greenwood, 1997.
Tom Sine	*Cease Fire: Searching for Sanity in America's Culture Wars.* Grand Rapids: Eerdemans, 1995.
Judith Stacey	*In the Name of the Family: Rethinking Family Values in the Postmodern Age.* Boston: Beacon Press, 1996.
Jean Stefancic and Richard Delgado	*No Mercy: How Conservative Think Tanks and Foundations Changed America's Social Agenda.* Philadelphia: Temple University Press, 1996.
Cal Thomas	*The Things That Matter Most.* New York: HarperCollins, 1994.
Joseph Turow	*Breaking Up America: Advertisers and the New Media World.* Chicago: University of Chicago Press, 1997.
John K. Wilson	*The Myth of Political Correctness.* Durham, NC: Duke University Press, 1995.
Alan Wolfe	*One Nation, After All: What Middle-Class Americans Really Think About God, Country, Family, Racism, Welfare, Immigration, Homosexuality, Work, the Right, the Left, and Each Other.* New York: Viking, 1998.

INDEX

media, 81
  bad language in, 86
  could be teaching vehicle, 43
  incivility in, 88
  and popularity of American movies, 91-92
  positive aspects of, 90
  role in politics, 34-35
  secularism in, 46
    confusion caused by, 47-50
    values portrayed in, 93
  see also popular culture
Medicare, 131
Medved, Michael, 91
Metropolitan Opera of New York, 182
Michelman, Kate, 161
militia movement, 40-41
minorities, 98, 105, 146
  see also African Americans; Hispanic
    Americans; Asian Americans
Mollenkott, Virginia Ramey, 36
morality, 29
  belief in God necesary for, 111, 113-14
  complexity of, 63
  decline in, 54-57, 71
    exaggerations about, 60, 61, 65-68
    egalitarianism ignored by, 62, 63-64
  and need for absolute values, 112, 120
  as separate from God, 115, 117, 119
    according to Plato, 116, 118
    and other philosophers, 120
  see also religion
Morgan, Edward P., 78
Morris, Scott M., 44
Morrison, Jim, 70, 71
multiculturalism, 27, 140, 146-47, 148
  and art, 185-86
  impetus for, 154
  negative effects of, 155-56
  and politics of race, 151
  see also bilingual education; diversity
Muslim extremists, 129

Nathanson, Bernard, 168
Nation, 134
National Abortion and Reproductive
  Rights Action League (NARAL), 161
National Academy of Sciences, 178
National Association for Bilingual
  Education (NABE), 175, 178
National Association for the Education of
  Young Children, 180
National Catholic Reporter, 131
National Conference of Catholic Bishops,
  133
National Council of Churches, 137
National Endowment for the Arts (NEA),
  73, 74

elimination of is desirable, 181, 187
inability to change, 186
inappropriate use of grants by, 183-85
need for federal support, 191
need to retain, 188, 192
successes of, 189, 190
National Endowment for the Humanities,
  56
National Organization for Women, 39
National Press Club, 191
National Review, 165
National Right to Life Committee, 40
Nazism, 20, 21, 129
Nelson, Cary, 103, 104
New Christian Right, 28
New Dictionary of Theology, 37
New Republic magazine, 22
Newton, Isaac, 45
New York magazine, 104
New York Times, 20, 21, 23, 179, 185
Nicaraguan Contras, 135
Nietzsche, Friedrich, 113
Nisbet, Robert, 71
Nolan, James L., 22
North Atlantic Treaty Organization
  (NATO), 92
North, Oliver, 27, 28
Nye, Joseph, 93
NYPD Blue, 86

O.J. Simpson trial, 55
Oklahoma bombing, 40
Orren, Gary, 67
Orwell, George, 98, 155
Ostling, Richard, 48, 49

Percy, Walker, 20
Peter Hart Research Associates, 83
Peterson, Sally, 180
Philadelphia, Pennsylvania, 57
Phoenix Art Museum, 186
Pinckney, Charles, 186-87
Planned Parenthood, 161, 162, 163
Plato, 103, 116
polarization of society, 17, 23-25, 30, 31,
  33-34
  as delusion, 66-67
  exaggeration about, 26
    dangers of, 29
    and rhetoric, 27-28, 32-33, 35
  and fear of authoritarianism, 22
  and realignment of social divisions, 31
political activism, 30, 33, 35
  is needed to encourage interest in
    politics, 32
  and need to strengthen political parties,
    34